THE ARCHITECTURE OF A PROVINCIAL SOCIETY

Houses of Bruce County, Ontario 1850-1900

Ruth Cathcart

Photography by Charles van den Ouden

THE RED HOUSE PRESS

CANADIAN CATALOGUING IN PUBLICATION DATA
Cathcart, Ruth, 1932-
          The architecture of a provincial society:
houses of Bruce County, Ontario 1850-1900

Includes bibiliographial references and index.
ISBN 0-9681375-1-2

  1. Architecture, Domestic – Ontario – Bruce (County) –
History. 2. Historic buildings – Ontario – Bruce (County)
3. Bruce (Ont.: County) – History – 19th century. I. Title.

NA7242.O5C36 1999   728'.09713'21   C99-901202-9

Copyright © 1999 Ruth Cathcart
Published by The Red House Press, Box 927, Wiarton, Ontario N0H 2T0
Phone (519) 534-2439   Fax (519) 534-3228 Email: cathcart@log.on.ca

Produced by Ampersand Printing, Guelph, Ontario

Front cover: *The Thomson/Holliday House*
Back cover: *The Henry Cargill House (top)*
               The George Brockie House (bottom)

DEDICATION

To the owners of these historic houses who, in undertaking responsibility for them, are saving our architectural heritage.

TABLE OF CONTENTS

*Because readers will not yet be familiar with the new boundaries and names of recently amalgamated municipalities, the former designations, above, have been used to identify townships, towns and villages in Bruce County.

For the record: the townships of St. Edmunds, Lindsay, and Eastnor and the village of Lion's Head have been amalgamated as the *Municipality of Northern Bruce Peninsula*. Albemarle, Wiarton, and Sauble Beach are now called the *Town of South Bruce Peninsula*. The *Municipality of Arran-Elderslie* includes Paisley, Tara and Chesley. The *Town of Saugeen Shores* is the new name for the amalgamated municipalities of Saugeen Township, Port Elgin and Southampton. *Municipality of Brockton* comprises the townships of Brant and Greenock and the town of Walkerton. The townships of Huron and Kinloss are now known as the *Township of Huron-Kinloss*. The townships of Kincardine and Bruce, the village of Tiverton and the town of Kincardine are now referred to as the *Township of Kincardine-Bruce-Tiverton*. The townships of Carrick and Culross and the villages of Mildmay and Teeswater have been combined to form the *Municipality of South Bruce*.

Acknowledgements

I recognize with deepest gratitude the help I have received from the following:

Mary Witky – Chesley librarian; John Weichel – local historian Southampton; Shirley MacDonald – Ripley librarian; Linda Kerr – Teeswater librarian; Velda Douglas, local historian, Teeswater; Rita Collins; Mary Leggett; June Daniels; Eldon Roppel – local historian, Tiverton; Alvin Comiter – photographer, Halifax; Judy & Ken Thompson; Margaret Howard; Terry Murphy; Vicky Cooper – Registrar, Bruce County Museum & Archives; Laurene Good; Bruce Krug.

Three copy editors/proof readers have saved me from the legion of errors which marched across the pages of my manuscript. They are Mary Ann Hogbin of the Ginger Press bookstore in Owen Sound; Andrew Armitage, chief librarian of the Owen Sound and North Grey Union Library; Colin Cathcart, of Kiss & Cathcart, Architects, New York City and Associate Professor of Architecture, Fordham University. The book was produced with admirable efficiency by the team of Mike McDonald, Carolyn Klymko and the staff of Ampersand Printing in Guelph, Ontario.

Travelling through the beautiful countryside of Bruce County with professional photographer Charles van den Ouden, to record the houses in this volume on film, was an unforgettable experience. His good humour saw us through wrong turns and retracing of steps with barely perceptible grimaces. His images tell the stories of the houses as surely as the text does.

Finally, I wish to acknowledge the loving kindness and enthusiastic support of my husband, Murray Cathcart.

Introduction

When Bruce County was opened for settlement – between 1850 and 1860 – it filled rapidly. The sons and daughters of established farm families in counties farther south were attracted by the promise of free fifty acre land grants and the opportunity to buy an adjoining fifty acres. There was a constant flow of immigrants from Britain – mainly Scotland – but also some from Germany. The "Big Land Sale" in Southampton, September 27, 1854, confirmed the attraction of this part of western Ontario to settlers. $60,000 worth of business was done in the first two days.

Bruce County sent legions of its people westward when the railway opened the prairies for settlement. By 1900 the great migration was fully underway. The federal government's homesteading plan in the west held out an inviting inducement which led to full ownership of 160 acres. Large families in the Bruce were multiplying and their 100 acre farms could no longer sustain second and third generations. The population of Bruce county declined from about 51,000 in 1901 to 41,500 in 1941.

Today, it is apparent that there is a "resettlement" of Bruce County by urban refugees – those who have permanently migrated from southern cities and those who are weekend migrants to their homes here. We are told that in the Bruce Peninsula more than 50% of property owners are urban migrants (Bruce County Historical Society Yearbook 1975). The present population of Bruce County is about 61,500.

The most numerous of the original settlers were the Scots who have defined the character of Bruce County. There is a plethora of unamalgamated Presbyterian churches and United Churches (in which the Presbyterians were persuaded to join with the Methodists and Congregationalists in the 1920s). During the pioneer era Gaelic was the dominant language. The 109 families from the Isle of Lewis who settled in Huron Township in the fall of 1852 spoke Gaelic almost exclusively. Presbyterian worship services were conducted in the Gaelic language through the 1930s in Ripley and Tiverton.

Of course, the settlers encountered unimagined hardships. Most were not woodsmen and had to quickly acquire that skill in order to clear the forest for their homesteads. Alexander Greig (see p. 20) tells in his diary of "beavering" around the perimeter of a tree with his axe in the vain hope that it would fall in the direction he willed it. However, he soon developed the skill to built his family a durable log shanty which still stands. Most immigrants to the new land were a determined, hardy people focussed on accomplishing their dreams and, it must be said, there wasn't much to distract them. They built their log shanties and dealt with life as they encountered it.

In *Pioneer Days at Guelph and the County of Bruce*, David Kennedy writes, "The Indians used to come up to our shanty and stand outside by the door and halloo loudly, and when we would leave our work to see what was wanted, they would say *tobacco*, and when we told them we had none, they would then pat on their stomachs, and say *buckity*. That meant that they were hungry and if we had any bread we would give them something to eat. They were always peaceable and quietly disposed." (It should also be noted that the aboriginal people shared their insights with the pioneers and gave them practical assistance.)

Kennedy's worst experiences seem to have centred around plagues of mice. He writes, "We used every conceivable means of destroying them . . . and sometimes we would get the lend of a cat for a few days, but nothing seemed to have any effect . . . so daring were they that if we left the table a moment to fetch the tea or coffee pot from the hearth, they would come and snatch our ham or bread from our plate and run away with it in a moment. My brother often caught them with his hands and killed them by the dozen while sitting at the table."

On the other hand, Bruce County had great natural assets. Aside from the valuable lumber taken from the land, there were vast shoals of fish in the waters of Georgian Bay and Lake Huron. W. M. Brown MD, writing in *The Queen's Bush*, noted "The advance of a shoal of fish in Lake Huron was indicated by a wave of light advancing along the waters shorewards." Passenger pigeons were so numerous near the lakes in the Wiarton region they could be batted down by children with sticks.

Bruce County is fortunate in having its own historian in Norman Robertson who published *History of the County of Bruce* in 1906. He was county treasurer from 1887 until 1924. In his spare time he carried out countless interviews with elderly settlers to which he added data from his own research. His account of the times is authentic and reliable and every household in Bruce County should own a copy of his book. (It has been regularly reprinted by the Bruce County Historical Society and is available at the county museum and area book shops.)

The other inimitable resource for history-minded readers is the Bruce County Museum & Archives located in the town of Southampton. The staff, supported by an enlightened county government and a large body of volunteers, has been tireless in gathering, referencing and storing the evidence of our past.

The domestic architecture of Bruce County is the equal of that in any area of Ontario. And, although it could never be characterized as a wealthy county, it is a well-known axiom that poverty is the best friend of preservation. Many of the early houses have changed little over the hundred or more year since they were built. Consequently we have a relatively unaltered view of what the settlers built for themselves.

Many more houses, of course, have been ruined by thoughtless changes made in the name of "modernization". Handsome, original windows have been replaced with inauthentic aluminum or plastic-framed windows. Chimneys have been torn down to be replaced by stainless steel pipes. Exteriors have been reclad with materials completely alien to the original materials of wood, brick and stone. Modern decks and picture windows deface front elevations.

This brings us to the message of this book. The conservation of our historic buildings is a subject to be taken seriously by today's society. These buildings represent in the clearest terms our origins as a nation, our transformation as a people. Heritage houses are compelling symbols of beauty and pride – history made visible. They are objects of value which have stood for one hundred to one hundred and fifty years and, with a modicum of care, they will stand for many more.

The houses chosen for inclusion in this volume, as in its companion, *How Firm a Foundation – Historic Houses of Grey County*, satisfied certain criteria. The first criterion is that of age. The older the house the more interest it holds for the historian and the more important is its existence today within the community. The second criterion has to do with aesthetic considerations. Is the design of the house pleasing? Is it well-sited? Is the craftsmanship high in quality?

The third criterion poses the most difficulty. It is authenticity. Old houses are bound to change, to evolve over the decades to meet the needs of new owners. Services such as plumbing and heating are updated as technology advances. More space is needed as families enlarge. Worn-out elements of buildings will need replacing – rooves, windows, verandahs. There are some old houses which are admirably suited to conversion for other uses – apartments, office space, public institutions. Nevertheless, modifications to heritage buildings can be accomplished in a sympathetic manner if there is a basic understanding of the idea of architectural integrity. Those old houses which have retained their original interest, charm and history have been included in this collection.

Historical relevance is an important criterion. What does the house tell us about the lives of the people who built it? How does the design express the character of its builder/owner, his social position and values? How does it express the space needs of the family, the availability of materials, the pattern books in circulation at the time, and the skills of the builder?

Finally, an effort was made to distribute the chosen houses over all of the geographic are of Bruce County – a county which stretches 150 kilometres from north to south – and to demonstrate ethnic-based differences in design and construction. The scope of any book of this type must be limited by practical limitations of space and cost, which means that worthy houses have been omitted. To their owners I offer my sincere regret.

Colin Cathcart, professor of architecture at Fordham University, has written about the heritage houses of this region, "This is vernacular architecture. There were few architects, luckily, and this means that many of these houses were more influenced by the good-sense design of sheds, barns, fences and hovels than they were by memories of the manor house twenty years prior in some faraway land. The styles are local ones, influenced only vaguely by English and American urban styles. They are your styles and nobody else's. And inventive frontier eclecticism is a rule to be celebrated, not some mutt to be excused."

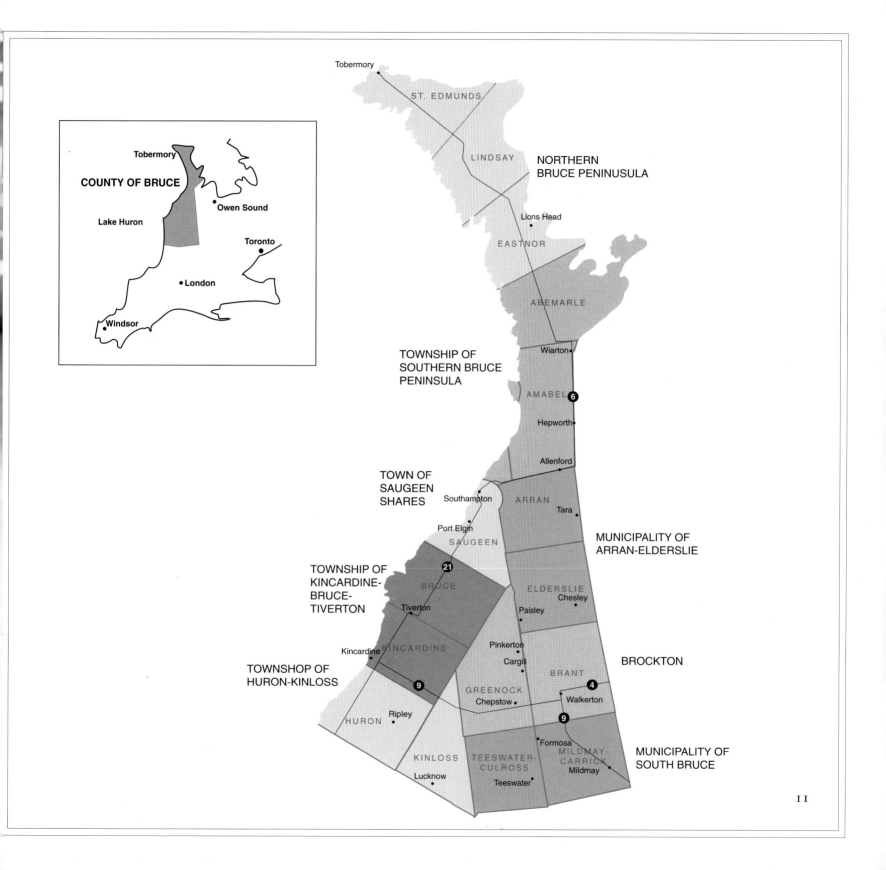

COUNTY OF BRUCE

Tobermory

Owen Sound

Lake Huron

Toronto

London

Windsor

Tobermory

ST. EDMUNDS

LINDSAY

NORTHERN
BRUCE PENINUSULA

Lions Head

EASTNOR

ABEMARLE

Wiarton

TOWNSHIP OF
SOUTHERN BRUCE
PENINSULA

AMABEL **6**

Hepworth

Allenford

TOWN OF
SAUGEEN
SHARES

Southampton

ARRAN

Tara

Port Elgin

SAUGEEN

MUNICIPALITY OF
ARRAN-ELDERSLIE

TOWNSHIP OF
KINCARDINE-
BRUCE-
TIVERTON

21

BRUCE

ELDERSLIE

Chesley

Paisley

Tiverton

Pinkerton

Cargill

BRANT

BROCKTON

Kincardine

KINCARDINE

4

TOWNSHOP OF
HURON-KINLOSS

9

GREENOCK

Walkerton

Chepstow

9

Ripley

HURON

MUNICIPALITY OF
SOUTH BRUCE

Formosa

KINLOSS

TEESWATER-
CULROSS

MILDMAY-
CARRICK

Lucknow

Teeswater

Mildmay

11

Albemarle Township

"HUGHENDEN" THE CARVER/WHICHER HOUSE   1883
Albemarle Township   Kribs Road, Village of Colpoys Bay

According to *Albemarle – A History of the Township*, Ernest Carver, a Master of Arts from Jesus College, Cambridge emigrated in 1881 to this property, which he bought from Ephraim Cross, its pioneer owner. The house was built for him by sawmiller, John Wood. Carver set out to become a "gentleman" farmer; trying his hand at stock raising, fruit tree growing and bee keeping – without noticeable success at any of these endeavors. His real interests seem to have been reading, music and especially chess, which he often played by correspondence. In fact, he won the Chess Correspondence Association of Ontario championship in 1930. Carver named the house *Hughenden* after the home of the same name belonging to Benjamin Disraeli, prime minister of England and a family friend.

Mrs. Ernest Carver's niece, Jean Battersby from Walkerville (now part of Windsor), spent several summers at *Hughenden* where she met Carl Whicher. When they were married in 1917 they bought the property from the Carvers, who then retired to Wiarton. Carl and Jean Whicher lived in this house for sixty-six years. One of their family of six children, Charles Henry "Harry" Whicher and his wife Joyce now reside here.

The Whicher family is descended from Henry and Harriet Whicher who came from Haldimand County to Colpoy's Bay in 1870. Individual members of this distinguished family have served their community as merchant, sawmiller, reeve, clerk of the township, Member of the Provincial Legislature and Member of Parliament.

The house itself, is the embodiment of the settler's dream animated by the memory of what he left behind. The dream was achieved by those who quickly made their fortunes in the new land or those who arrived with cash in their pockets – instant civilized stability. *Hughenden* is large, built of solid brick, well lit by generous windows and above all displays a rational symmetry in its design.

Amabel Township

The Shannon/Napier House c.1880
Amabel Township Concession 8 Part Lot 20

Fred Shannon's architect father, Frederick Senhen (1810-1893) and mother, Caroline Reimenach (1822-1893) were immigrants to Canada from Germany. They left from Bremen bound for New York City in 1857 with their two children. From New York they continued by covered wagon to Kitchener, a German settlement in Upper Canada; then on to Goderich, Southampton, and finally Amabel Township. Fred Shannon Jr., born in 1860, was one of four more children who made their appearance after the family arrived in the new land. He received the Crown Patent to the land on which his house was built in 1880. (A Patent is a document from the sovereign, conferring sole title to the land in question.)

The veneer brick farmhouse is a model of fine proportions and simplicity. Its entrance, round-arched gable window, and raised brickwork in the quoins, give it a timeless, classic air. Segmental arches give a slight "lift" to the lower floor, boosting the effect of the full round arch in the gable. The space behind the brick veneer is filled with gravel and cement – sometimes referred to as "grout" in this region. Interior walls are finished with lath and plaster. The summer kitchen, built by the Loucks around 1920, is a solid brick structure.

Alexander and Mary Loucks were descendants of United Empire Loyalists from New York state who had been given land near Kingston by the government of the United Canadas after the War of 1812. Eventually, they came west to Bruce County and bought this rather isolated property about 1900. It remains in the family today through Laney Loucks Napier and her husband Walter Napier and is now owned by Allan and Rita Napier.

THE JAMES RUSHTON HOUSE   1877

Amabel Township   Concession D Lot 6

T he mortar in this rough fieldstone house has been carefully scored to give the impression of stones laid in a regular pattern. In reality, the stones are extremely varied in colour, shape and size. The austere symmetry regularizes the proportions of the house, while the carefully segmented arches above the windows and the lacy gingerbread in the gothic centre gable give a sense of refinement to this pioneer structure.

This house was built by James Rushton, an early settler in this part of Bruce County. In fact, he is listed as one of only 124 settlers in Amabel Township in an 1867 directory. He came to Canada about 1860 with his wife Elizabeth and daughters Sarah and Margaret. Five more children were born in quick succession. Rushton received the Crown Patent for his 164 acres in June 1875 and built this pretty house in 1877. In the early days of settlement this generous family lent their ample house for community meetings and dances.

The Taylor/Wain House   c.1880
Amabel Township   Main and Elizabeth Streets, Allenford.

The village of Allenford was named for James Allen (1826-1896), who came to be respectfully known over a wide area as "Squire Allen". Born in County Fermanagh, Ireland, the son of James and Elizabeth H. Allen, he came to Canada in 1832. He settled in Amabel Township in 1857 and with his wife Elizabeth, raised a large family including an adopted girl orphaned by shipwreck on the Great Lakes. He was a merchant and a member of the first and every succeeding Council of Amabel until his death. For thirteen consecutive years of that time he was its Reeve, retiring voluntarily in 1880. James Allen was Indian Agent for the Chippewa Hill Band. When he died the Chippewas marched beside his hearse singing "Shall We Gather by the River". He was also a friend and trusted advisor to Canada's first Prime Minister, Sir John A. Macdonald.

Albert Allen, a son, has written in *Green Meadows and Golden Sands – the History of Amabel Township* about his father's charity. "I said to him one day, 'I never see you making a record of these endless outgoing of supplies – food and seed grain etc.' He replied in a low voice, 'Son, I do not make or want to make any record of the help I am able to give struggling members of a common family. I want nothing to remind me or them of these, their worst days. Should they become able to pay something, I would not hurt their feelings by refusing.'"

This house, in James Allen's Allenford, built for Dr. Archibald Taylor, became home and office to a succession of physicians. When George Wain (1863-1948) became Clerk of Amabel Township in 1915, a post he kept for thirty-three years, he bought the house. His father, George Wain Sr., had come to Amabel from Lincolnshire, England in the 1850s and married Ann McTaggert. He drowned when he was only twenty-nine years of age while attempting to cross the Sauble River with a load of supplies in March, 1864. George Wain Jr. married Emma Rowe in 1900 and they raised a family of five in this house.

The Taylor/Wain house has an appealing air because of its decorated gables, patterned brickwork in mellow shades of red and buff, semi-circular transom above the "suicide" door over the verandah, and bay windows. The brick "surgery" to one side of the building lends a happy informality to the ensemble.

THE ALEXANDER GREIG HOUSE 1861

Amabel Township   Concession 25 Lots 14, 15, 16

Alexander Greig (1832-1896) and his bride, Helen Galloway (1832-1905) came from their home in Fifeshire, Scotland to Bruce County in 1857. They settled in Amabel township in what came to be known as the Greig Settlement.

The story of their first years in Bruce County was written by Mr. Greig a few years before his death and reprinted in Norman Robertson's *History of the County of Bruce*. Greig tells of the family's surprise and disappointment when they arrived in Wiarton to find it existed in name only. The only settler in the locality, William Bull, was absent when they arrived and the place seemed to them, "a lone and vast wilderness". Mr. Bull helped them cut a road through the bush to their lots. Because they were inexperienced it took them four or five weeks to construct their first shelter, a log shanty. A few years later they built this stone house. The Greig family lives here to this day.

Alexander Greig soon learned the skills of a woodsman and, by the following midsummer, eleven of his acres were ready for logging. In the fall of 1858 he threshed twenty-five bushels of wheat with a flail and ground it in a coffee mill. It was not until the early 1860s that Mr. Greig received cash for any produce grown on his farm, an experience common to all in early settlement days. Because shops were so remote and cash was limited, even a sewing needle had great value. The community sewing needle was always threaded with red wool before it was passed on to the next user so that it would be less likely to be lost.

This simple structure possesses an indefinable charm. The warm-hued stones are random in size, ranging from tiny to huge. The corners are emphasized by cut quoins. A cheerful note is added by the scarlet painted wood trim on the wide eaves, around the windows, and the doorway which links the brick addition to the original stone structure. The bay window is said to be an exact replica of the one in the family home in Scotland. It is difficult to imagine a more beguiling house.

ALEXANDER GREIG FAMILY C. 1890

20

Arran Township

THE GEORGE SPENCE HOUSE   1890   (date stone)

Arran Township   Concession 13 Lot 31

Behold, the quintessential 19th century Ontario house. Built of red brick in a variation of the common bond pattern (technical terms such as common bond are defined in the glossary), its design elements include one-and-a-half storeys, symmetrical openings, gable-end roof, bargeboard outlining the gables, a "gothic" in the centre-front of the roof and, above all, decorative brickwork which is highlighted by the use of white paint. (The brickwork departs from the traditional in the strange segmental arches with ogee voussoirs and alternate painted extrados over the front door and windows.) Black shutters, door and roof complete a picture of a crisp, confident, composed structure.

George Spence occupied this land as early as 1852. He received the Crown Patent in 1866 and passed the property on to his son, Frederick, in 1897.

Brant Township

THE ALEXANDER KERR HOUSE   C.1870
Brant Township   Concession 3 SDR Lot 66

Alexander Kerr (1816-1896) was born a Scot. He came to Brant Township in the earliest days of its settlement. His name appears in the 1851 census as the owner of Lots 66, 67 and 68. Kerr obtained the Crown deed to this lot in 1865 and built his house soon after. His descendants remained on this property until 1909. The present owners, the Poechmans, have lived and worked here since 1921. Linus Poechman and his wife, Helen Weiler, farmed and carried on a market garden operation here while raising six children. Their son, Allan and his wife, Joan Tanner, and their family continue the family tradition.

These two well-rooted families symbolize the stability and the constancy of Bruce County people. Their homes are expressions of their steadfastness. After more than thirteen decades this house is as solid and true as the day it was built. It is made of stone from the fields, the windows are many and large, and the entrance is expansive and welcoming. The charm of the building arises from the texture and colour of the exterior walls and the simple symmetry of its design.

St. Peter's Lutheran Church Manse   1872

Brant Township   Concession 4 Lot 29

A thriving church community once existed here. The first congregation of St. Peter's Lutheran Church was formed in 1860 and a log church was built in 1862. Mission festivals were once-a-year highlights for many decades when three services of worship were held during the special day. Lunch and dinner were provided for as many as eight hundred Lutherans, many of whom had travelled from neighbouring congregations to share in the festival.

A fine brick church, built in 1869, was closed in 1954 and sold. With the proceeds, a fence was erected around the cemetery and a cairn was built in honour of the pioneers buried here.

The manse was built for the family of the Rev. Wilhelm Mackensen (1833-1897) in 1872. He arrived in Brant from Badenhausen, Germany in the fall of 1867 after crossing the Atlantic by sail in seven weeks. Sophie Scholvien (1839-1929) arrived from Hanover, Germany the following year by steamboat. They were married in 1868 and raised a family of ten children.

The manse remains an example of the generic Ontario dwelling-place. Only the porch and the balcony above it have been altered. Red brick is laid in a common bond pattern. Buff brick is used to suggest quoins at the house corners and to make a pattern under the eaves and around the pointed-arch window. A gable, centering the front roof, provides space for a window to give light to the upper half storey. The doorway is refined by a glazed transom and sidelights. Above it is an inscription in German taken from verse three of the fourteenth chapter of Hosea in the Christian Bible.

This classic Ontario house structure has its antecedents in the small Renaissance house of western Europe. In Ontario it has become an architectural icon, a fitting representation of our early history.

"Viewfield" The Alexander Shaw House c.1880

Brant Township   Concession 1 NDR Lot 34

This ample Victorian house exhibits a strong classicism in its design – especially in the use of pedimented gables, and brickwork which suggests dentils at the wall tops and the belt course. The decorative chimneys, brackets under the wide eaves, solid quoining, and French verandahs add more conventional high Victorian components to the design.

The interior of the house follows the tradition of the great houses of Bruce County. Ceilings on the main floor are twelve feet in height. Mouldings are wide and complex in profile. The staircase rises in a graceful curve from a spacious foyer. Many fireplaces add warmth. Two of these, worthy of special mention, were saved from the family seat in Wigan, Lancashire, England, when a section of the building was demolished early in this century. One fireplace dates to the time of Elizabeth I and includes stunning hearth tiles and inlaid woodwork. The other is made of ebonized wood in the Tudor style inlaid with artistic tile-work bearing family initials.

The property first belonged to Archibald Todd who received the Crown Patent in 1853. He became Brant Township's first clerk – 1879 to 1882. Born in Londonderry, Ireland in 1798 he came to Canada in 1832 and then moved on to Brant in 1849. The Todd family helped to build Walkerton, the county town.

Alexander Shaw, born in 1833 in Ramsay Township, Lanark County, was educated in Perth, Upper Canada. He came to Kincardine in 1858 to practice law. While there he raised a volunteer militia company at the time of American conflict with Britain over the "Trent Affair".

He moved on to Walkerton around 1862 where he practiced in the firm Shaw & Robertson. He was appointed county solicitor in 1867 – a post he held until 1906. Anna Robertson became his wife and they raised a family of five sons and two daughters.

In 1878 Shaw entered politics when, as a Conservative candidate in the federal riding of South Bruce, he defeated the Honourable Edward Blake. He was defeated by Blake in 1882 and was defeated again in 1890 when he ran as an Independent in Centre Bruce.

Shaw was directly responsible for persuading the government of John A. Macdonald to cancel the timber-cutting privileges of large lumber companies on land owned by the settlers of the Bruce Peninsula – a desperately needed reform.

In later years Alexander Shaw, KC contributed to the community when he led a group to establish and administer Bruce County's Children's Aid Society.

Bruce Township

THE TIVERTON SCHOOLHOUSE
Bruce Township   7 McKay Street, Tiverton

This solid brick building, once a schoolhouse, is now an apartment building. As a schoolhouse, it accommodated two classrooms for grades one to eight downstairs and two classrooms upstairs for what used to be known as "continuation school" – grades nine to twelve. It ceased to be used as a school in 1949.

The Tiverton schoolhouse was built by George Clelland in 1875. He was a lumber mill owner and contractor who also built the Tiverton Town Hall and many houses, not only in Tiverton but in nearby villages, including Kincardine.

George Clelland (1843-1939) was born in Boghead, Lanarkshire, Scotland and came to Canada as a young man. He married Margaret Semple (1846-1912) also of Boghead.

When he was fifty-eight years old Clelland was forced to make good the value of a friend's estate when the co-executor skipped town with the assets. This cost him his life savings. Discouraged, he left Tiverton for Toronto where he lived to a ripe old age. When asked why he thought he had achieved such longevity he said, "I don't smoke, I go to bed early and I don't wear silk stockings."

The balanced facade of the building features a slightly projected centre bay with a distinctive recessed entry. Solid brick quoins outline the bay and the corners of the building. Several bolt ends of re-enforcing rods are visible on the exterior elevations. The use of rods to support and strengthen walls is not an uncommon sight in old buildings. The character of the building has been left intact by a sensitive conversion of school building to apartment house.

The village of Tiverton was established in the late 1850s. By 1860 its population numbered 550 persons. The Bruce Nuclear Power Development facility is located nearby.

THE JOB CARR HOUSE   1885 (date stone)

Bruce Township   Lot H Concession 13

Job Carr bought this property from Fred Holtz in 1867. The Bruce Township census of 1871 lists Carr as English, twenty-four years of age and head of a household consisting of his sister Rhoda, thirty-five years and her child Herbert, five years. Local history has it that Carr, carrying his nephew on his back, walked with his sister from Owen Sound to his property – a distance of about thirty miles. This handsome stone house was built in 1885.

    Bruce Township – Tales and Trails, a history of the area, describes Job Carr as "a rather mysterious character, with the appearance and manner of an English gentleman who never worked yet was never short of money. Neighbours still recall his English country garden with its quince, walnut trees, flowering shrubs, holly and many strange and unfamiliar plants. Whenever flowers were needed for the church, he would cut a gorgeous bouquet. There were stories of a connection to Royalty; he was known to receive mail from England and make trips back across the ocean. Carr dismissed the neighbours' children as "Devil's Imps", a name they may have earned as he was a favourite target for pranks. His fruit trees attracted those who mischievously helped themselves. He paid youngsters twenty-five cents for a dead groundhog; the carcass went into the bottom of the hole when Job planted a tree, shrub or rhubarb."

    Rita Collins, daughter of the subsequent owner of the property, Arthur Collins, remembers that Job Carr walked everywhere, disdaining a horse and buggy. She says his house was almost completely hidden from the road by the luxuriant growth of his garden. A peacock was kept to add an exotic note to the picture of an English gentleman's country domain.

    Job Carr left his beloved home and garden to his nephew and wife, Herbert and Elizabeth Carr in 1929. They, in turn, sold it to the Arthur Collins family who lived and worked here for 40 years.

THE HUGH MCEWEN HOUSE   C.1870

Bruce Township   79 Queen Street, Tiverton

The McEwens, Peter (1816-1908) and Janet (1815-1901), came to Canada from Perthshire, Scotland in 1831. She was the daughter of Hugh McCallum and Catherine Campbell who eloped and came to Canada in 1817 because her father, the Marquis of Breadalbane of Castle Tay, disapproved of her marriage.

Peter and Janet's son Hugh, born in 1841, was the builder of this house. He owned a mill and a dry goods store in Tiverton in partnership with his brother John.

The house is an unchanged example of the best of Ontario vernacular domestic architecture. It is a one-and-a-half storey Ontario Cottage, enhanced by a one-storey frontispiece which anchors a two-part verandah with an awning roof. What sets the Hugh McEwen house apart from any other in Bruce County is the window in the large front gable. It is glazed in the Regency style in a tripartite opening which is set back into the wall. It gives the house a air of gentle distinction. One hopes that the common depredations of historic wood windows – that is, covering them over as if they had never existed, or replacing them with modern characterless windows – will never occur, especially in this case.

Carrick Township

THE JACOB ROSSEL HOUSE 1872 (date stone)
Carrick Township   Concession 15 Part Lot 30

In considering the components of an imposing historic house such as this one, we are drawn to the conclusion that site is vitally important. The building is set on a slight rise among extensive gardens and is framed by mature, healthy trees. It is fully exposed to the road, not half hidden by the garden growth. Other farm buildings do not encroach on the house or overwhelm it. All of the structures form a cohesive whole.

The structure itself is made of limestone, which has acquired the patina and texture of age. Its size and mass indicate the generosity of spirit and resources of the builder. Its proportions are harmonious, a key to beauty in architecture. The building has retained its personality, its character, its spirit because it has been faithfully maintained over the years.

The house was erected by Jacob and Katherine Rossel (the spelling of the surname as it appears in the early Land Registry documents). The Crown Patent for the 123 acre lot was awarded to the Rossels in 1866. Four generations of the family, headed by Jacob, John, Clarence and Warren have owned and worked the farm over the past 133 years. A cider mill on the property, first powered by a 1914 Buick engine, is still in operation. Warren and Shirley Russell's sons, John, Clare and Greg carry on a venerable family tradition in the business of farming, apple cider making and maintenance of the farmstead.

The Gregory Weber House 1873 (date stone)

Carrick Township   Concession 10 Part Lot 34

Gregory Weber obtained the Crown Patent for his 100 acre lot in 1866. It remained in the family until 1972.

The building is an especially fine example of a German fieldstone house of five bays – that is, five openings in the front elevation. The generous dimensions of the front entrance include an elegantly glazed transom and sidelights. The second half-storey is lit by a pointed arch window and delicate bargeboard outlines the roof. The verandah has been faithfully restored, although with a straight roof rather than the awning roof which is shown in a 1914 photograph.

Carrick township received two groups of German settlers after its 1852 survey. Some came directly from Europe but many more arrived from the Kitchener-Waterloo area. These immigrants from Waterloo County to Bruce County were sons and daughters of the pioneers who had settled that region in the 1820s.

THE ROMAN CATHOLIC CONVENT   c.1872

Carrick Township   Village of Formosa

A large proportion of the early settlers of Carrick Township were from Germany or Alsace and of the Roman Catholic persuasion. This is especially true of the village of Formosa. Formosa's splendid Church of the Immaculate Conception was built in 1883 around the old frame church in which services continued to be held while construction of the new building was underway. The frame building was then dismantled and carried out piece by piece. Stone for the new church was quarried locally under the direction of craftsman Nicholas Durrer. The church has seating for nine hundred and a spire which reaches 180 feet heavenward.

This fine brick house was built as a convent in 1872 by Francis X. Messner. He had come to Formosa with his brother Anthony in 1862. They established several business enterprises – a general store, a bank and a brewery. Messner was a prominent Liberal and on one occasion received the unanimous nomination in East Bruce for the House of Commons, an honour which he declined. (*History of the County of Bruce*). Although Messner later suffered business reverses which affected many villagers financially, he was always remembered with affection for his stalwart character and helpfulness.

The three bays of the brick house rise through the roofline to produce interesting gables – all lined with attractive bargeboard. The entrance is imposing because it is recessed and supplied with transom and sidelights. The door above may have opened onto a balconey at one time. The side bay window and decorative roof dormers add their grace notes to the composition.

THE CONRAD KAUFMAN HOUSE   1880 (date stone)
Carrick Township   Concession 8 Part Lot 34

The history of this farm property has been well-documented in *Historical Walks Through Carrick and Mildmay 1854-1984*. Conrad Kaufman purchased the land from the Crown in 1869 for $178. He married Anna C. Haberling and they had nine children. In 1880 Mr. Kaufman contracted with Henry Barlett, a stonemason from Neustadt, to build his stone house for $300. All the building materials came from the farm property. The deal included provision for a forty gallon barrel of whiskey for the sustenance of the construction crew. It was transported by a team of horses from the Seagrams distillery in Kitchener at a cost of $18.75.

It was necessary to use a gin pole, ropes, pulleys, and horses to lift heavy field stones from the ground to a scaffold and thence to the wall. The stones had been cracked by heating them in an intense fire, followed by a cooling off process and the use of a well-aimed sledge hammer, employed by the master craftsman.

The Conrad Kaufman house is typical in its proportions, dimensions, openings and roofline of the houses built by German immigrant settlers. Many such houses still grace the landscape in Carrick Township. Particularly notable in this example is the recessed front doorway which retains its original Regency-style glazing, the pointed-arch window and the delicate bargeboard and kingpin in the gable.

August Lantz, his wife Wilhemina Ortman, and their three children farmed here from 1912 till 1952. The present owners, Robert and Mildred Crawford, bought the property in 1960, raised their five children here and now are enjoying their retirement in this exceptional house.

The Hay/Schwalm House 1886 (name and date stone)
Carrick Township   3 Adam Street, Mildmay

The Village of Mildmay was established in the 1850s at the place where the settlers' trail, known as the Elora Road, crossed Otter Creek. The falls in the creek offered colonists energy to drive their mills. Mildmay was also blessed with a pure and copious supply of water which still serves the community. When the Grand Trunk Railway arrived in 1872 the town entered a boom cycle.

Alfred Hay, a blacksmith and builder, came to Mildmay about 1875, accomplishing much in his fourteen years before leaving for California. He built a good number of shops and houses including his own where he left his name and the date of construction imprinted in the window hood above the front porch.

In 1901 the property was transferred to the Roman Catholic Episcopal Corporation of the Diocese of Hamilton which ran a residence here for the teaching Sisters of Notre Dame until 1915. Many of the village residents were German Catholics who had already built a major church and a separate school.

Edward A., son of George Schwalm and his wife Emma Margaret Schwalm, acquired the house in 1926 and their descendants remained here until 1972. George and his brother Nicholas, had developed a large sawmill, and a building supplies and contracting business in Mildmay in 1880. Several generations of the family, including Edward A. and his son Edward William, expanded the business and eventually acquired extensive woodlots and woodcutting privileges on neighbouring farms. They were the local contractors for numerous buildings in the area. The sawmill was rebuilt after a disastrous fire in 1925. Firemen were at the scene for sixteen hours for which, we are told in the township history, they were paid thirty cents an hour.

The house is vernacular Italianate in style – with wide eaves, double brackets and neo-classical detailing over some of the windows. It presents a solid, prosperous facade to the community.

Chesley

The Dr. J.M. Stewart House   c.1890
Chesley   corner of Main Street & 3rd Street West

To discover this extraordinary building in a town which is isolated from any large urban centre and has a population of fewer than 2,000, is an unexpected and keen pleasure. Known as the "Doctor's House", it provided living quarters and offices for a succession of local physicians. Today the Stewart house serves as a senior citizens' centre.

Dr. Stewart, a graduate in medicine from Queen's University, came to Chesley in 1882. He bought this property the next year and had his house and office built by David Stephens in 1885. Stephens was a contractor and builder who operated the Chesley Planing Mill and Sash & Door factory which he founded in 1884. He employed about twenty men and built the Evangelical church and many of the fine old houses of Chesley and the surrounding district. Dr. Stewart and his wife raised their family of three sons and two daughters in Chesley. One son lost his life in WWI and another died later of battle wounds. As well as practicing medicine, Dr. Stewart served on the town council from 1887 till 1897 and then as reeve of the village from 1887 till 1901. Drs. Downing, Fraser and Dawson succeeded Dr. Stewart in this remarkably fine house.

Its style is described as "Richardsonian Romanesque" after the American architect, Henry Hobson Richardson (1838-1886). He was an original and, at the same time, a learned architect. His favourite style was a massive, masculine "Romanesque" which is faithfully represented in this large house. The round, three-storey tower with a rusticated limestone base is topped with a conical roof. One of the dormers on the south side of the house is artfully camouflaged by a Tudor-style facing rising through the roofline, a reference to Richardson's "Arts & Crafts" affiliations – as are the grouped windows in the front gable and the decorative shingling. The arched entrance is a direct reference to the "Romanesque" style associated with Richardson's name.

THE WELLINGTON KRUG HOUSE C.1885

Chesley   159 Main Street South

The Chesley Woollen Mills, established in 1885, were owned by James Grant who is thought to have built this house. It exhibits the intricacies of the late Queen Anne Style – multiple wall planes, roof intersections, gables and high decorative chimneys. One of its glories is an elaborate leaded-glass front door.

In 1914 Conrad Krug acquired the house. He was one of the founders of the Krug Furniture Company, reeve of the village in 1905-1906 and mayor of the town in 1907-1910. His son, Wellington Krug, continued to live here for many years.

For over one hundred years the Krug Furniture Company was the major industry in town. Brothers Conrad, Christian, John, William and George with their brother-in-law Henry Ankenman came to Chesley in 1886. Their company produced home and office furnishings from native woods such as maple and cherry, harvested from their own extensive woodlots. The sons of Christian Krug; Howard and Bruce, continued the business until 1987 when it was finally sold.

THE BECKER HOUSE   C.1890

Chesley   54   Third Street East

The bricks in this cottage, a building which appears to be tiny but stretches considerably to the rear, are laid in the common bond pattern, the most common pattern of solid brick masonry in the region. The contrasting buff brick of the segmental arches above the windows is also typical. Hundreds of these small brick houses were built throughout the region between 1875 and 1900.

It is the front and side external vestibules which pull this petite house out of the ordinary. They are in the late Victorian "Aesthetic Period" style in which diagonal patterning in wood was used for special effect. The round-headed windows of the front vestibule and classically inspired pilasters combined with the diagonal pattern add a note of gaiety to a plain and simple dwelling.

THE HENRY CARTER HOUSE   C.1881

Chesley   80 2nd Street South East.

Chesley has, in this house, its own fine example of the Italianate style of High Victorian architecture. Note the wide, panelled and dentilled frieze under the roof, and the decorative roof brackets, some of which are paired and some tripled. The tall, rectangular windows are also paired in the Italianate manner. Best of all is the repeating pattern of the hipped roofs as seen from the front elevation, a design feature of some sophistication. The angularity of the house is reinforced by raised brickwork outlining belt courses and corners. Inside, the ceilings are ten-and-a-half feet high on the main floor and ten feet high upstairs. The baseboards are thirteen inches deep.

Henry Carter, who had the house constructed by a builder named Stevens, was a Chesley merchant in hardware, stoves and tinware. He had formed a partnership with J.H. Elliot and they opened their store on main street in 1870.

The house is known locally as the "Andy King House" because of his family's later tenancy from 1931 to 1946. King was a drayman who transported goods and people to and from the train station after the arrival of the Grand Trunk Railway in 1881.

Culross Township

"OMEGA PLACE" THE CHARLES EWING HOUSE c.1900
Culross Township   12 Brownlee Street, Teeswater

Omega Place is a mate to its next door neighbour, which is named *Alpha Lodge*. They were built by brothers-in-law who not only lived side by side but were partners in business. The houses present mirror images of each other to the street. *Omega Place's* two-storey tower with its curving conical roof rises on the north side of the building, while *Alpha Lodge's* tower rises on its south side. Both buff brick houses are distinguished by wide eaves visually supported by decorative brackets, tall corbelled chimneys and enveloping verandahs with awning roofs punctuated by double dormer windows. The unknown builder has left a valuable legacy to the village which has been carefully preserved by subsequent owners.

Charles Ewing (1872-1937) and Mary Louise Ewing (1876-1967) lived here in the early part of the 20th century. Ewing was a partner with R.J. Mann, his brother-in-law, in a general store on the main street of the village.

The Village of Teeswater, named after its river, lies in the southern part of Bruce County. Its history as the commercial centre of Culross Township began in 1854 with the "Big Land Sale" in Southampton so often mentioned in these pages. This sale opened Bruce County to a flood of settlers. The usual pattern of development followed. A dam was built on the river providing power for a sawmill, gristmill and tannery. Retail commerce and professional services followed. Hotels were built to accommodate salesmen who came through by train. For the past many decades Teeswater has been known for its dynamic Agricultural Society and banner annual agricultural fair.

THE DAVID IRELAND HOUSE   c.1877

Culross Township   Concession 3 Lot 15

This trim, fieldstone farm house has considerable appeal, not only for what it is but because it has been meticulously maintained. The term house proud has a negative connotation of blind enslavement to "keeping" house. But perhaps the phrase can also mean the love of home, a particular house, and the acceptance of responsibility for preserving it. This building will stand for generations as a testament to the quality of its execution and the determination of succeeding owners to protect it.

A full description of the Ireland family and farm is found in *All our Yesterdays – a History of Culross Township 1854-1984*. David Alexander Ireland was born at Newry, Armagh County, Ireland in 1828. He and his brother and sister came to Culross in 1857. David obtained the Crown deed for his farm in 1866 and he built a log house just west of the present stone house. In 1869 he married Jane Whiteman. Their stone house measuring thirty-four by twenty-five feet was built in 1877. The walls are two feet thick at the bottom and eighteen inches at the top.

Robert and his wife, Lisseta MacDonald Ireland, succeeded his father, David, in 1905 and introduced new farming methods to the area. Next to undertake responsibility for the farm was Donald Ireland and his wife, Alberta Ferguson. Since Donald's death in 1979, sons David and Mark farm the property under the name "Albadon Farms".

THE IRA FULFORD HOUSE C.1885

Culross Township.   Just north of the village of Teeswater on Highway 4

This elegant house was built on property first claimed by Jessie Fulford in a Crown Patent dated 1863. It is of a design often seen in Bruce County and is classical in its symmetry. The front-facing slope of the hipped roof is centred by a gable within which a window is placed to light the interior of the attic. Three-sided bays add interest to the main floor facade. Such bays have the effect of breaking up exterior wall planes and adding variation and light to the interior.

Segmental-arch windows are articulated with brick voussoirs and dropped keystones. Raised quoins at the corners of the house are a feature of superior brickwork. The wooden porch is particularly ornamental with its slender columns and arched entry.

The Belden 1880 *Bruce County Atlas* tells us that the Jesse Fulford family was of United Loyalist descent, having settled in Connecticut and fought on the side of the British during the Revolutionary War. The family was then obliged to flee to Canada after American Independence. They settled in Elizabethtown, Upper Canada, in 1793. Ira Fulford, was born in 1830 and came to Culross Township in 1855 followed a year later by his father, Jesse. Ira became active in local affairs and served on the Teeswater council for some years.

Eastnor Township

THE LEITH/SHAW HOUSE c.1887

Eastnor Township   Hamlet of Spry Concession 3 WBR Part Lot 20

The first land sales in the central part of the Bruce Peninsula were recorded in 1862. However, there were very few settlers until the early 1870s. George Leith built his home and store in Spry in 1887. In the earlier years the store, operated by Robert and then George McMaster, supplied not only provisions but filled other community needs. The Stokes Bay Royal Mail stage coach, carrying mail and passengers from Wiarton to Stokes Bay, stopped here. Rooms and a stable were available. The store was the site of the first telephone between Spry and Lion's Head.

In 1924 W. E. Shaw and his wife Mildred purchased the property and removed the store building. Shaw became a trucker and clerk of Eastnor Township. After his death, Mildred worked as the caretaker of a one-room schoolhouse across the road (SS #2) and boarded some of the teachers.

The style of this house is commonly known as Carpenter Gothic because of the decorative and vaguely gothic details achieved by a builder in wood. Some of these details include diagonal and horizontal panels, decorative shingles, and spindles in the gables that have been retained in a restoration of the building by a descendent of the Shaw family. It is a handsome reminder of the people who opened the Bruce Peninsula to settlement.

Elderslie Township

THE HERRIOTT/OSWALD HOUSE C.1870

Elderslie Township   Concession 7 Lot 26

Most of our Ontario houses are vernacular in design. That is, their form, appearance, and layout reflect popular practice, and a common notion of "high style" at the time they are built. For obvious reasons, these houses are not architect-designed. At the time of settlement and for some time after, there were no architects in this region. Even if there had been, the cost of their services would have been well beyond the ability of most settlers to pay. The designs of early houses are reflections of the homes settlers left behind in England, Scotland, Ireland and in Germany.

This house may be characterized as vaguely Georgian in style, meaning that it is an adaptation of the style popular in Europe during the reign of the English King Georges in the eighteenth and early nineteenth centuries. It was built by a stone mason who translated his idea of house design from his homeland to Canada. The material for his house came from nearby fields and is admirably suited to the style.

Balance, rhythm and regularity, along with a scale of expression fitted to the station of the occupants, are the core ideas informing the Georgian style. The interior layout consists of a centre hall from which a staircase rises to the second floor. On both floors the rooms open from the centre hall. This layout is reflected in the exterior design which consists of the main entrance centered in the front facade and symmetrically placed windows on at least three sides of the building. The roof is referred to as a gable end. There is often a chimney rising from each end, supporting and serving rooms on either side of the centre hall.

Fieldstone houses such as this add lustre to our vernacular architecture. The masonry is remarkable. Here are semi-dressed stones for "quoining by colour" and at window and door surrounds, infilled with a crazy quilt of darker stones. This is a crazy quilt assembled with a calculating eye. Could this be a case of the provinces upstaging the staid city centres of culture?

John Halliday Herriott received the Crown Patent to this property in 1894. He must have settled it much earlier and built this fine house around 1870. In 1898 he sold the farm to John Oswald for $3,100. The Oswald family made this their home for many years.

The Thomson/Halliday House   1902

Elderslie Township   Concession 7 Lot 19

In 1870 Edward Thomson and his wife Ann Carruthers left Lanarkshire, Scotland for Canada. They bought this farm of ninety-nine acres – forty of which were cleared – and a log cabin from Forbes McCalder in 1871. They added a barn and this house. The property stayed within the Thomson family until 1962 when it was purchased by Charles F. Halliday. In 1976 the Hallidays received an award for the farm under the *Farmstead and Rural Improvement* initiative.

The large, fieldstone house has benefited from the careful addition of a broad staircase to a handsome front porch. The overall design of the house conforms to a commonly used L massing. This L allows for five gables – and gables, with their intersecting roof ridges and valleys, always add interest to house design. They also provide space for the bedroom half-storey with its sloping ceilings associated with our one-and-a-half storey houses.

THE DONALD REID HOUSE   c.1875

Elderslie Township   Concession 5 Lots 12 & 13

Here is the quintessential Ontario Gothic farmhouse, standing in an open field and framed by huge old poplar trees twice its size. The total effect of the house in its site is one of severe restraint. However, white-painted brickwork around the openings, the corners and the beltcourse adds a note of cheerfulness to the utterly simple design of the structure.

Peter Reid (1829-1896), a pioneer blacksmith, married Christena Taylor (1839-1925) in Paisley in 1860. The original blacksmith shop on the property is still intact and in use. This farm has been in the Reid family through the generations represented by Donald Reid, Wilfred Reid, and now Scot Reid.

This enduring family history and the vernacular architectural design of the house combine to tell a story of the character of rural Ontario. It is a story of the steadiness, resolve and optimism of the first settlers, and their descendants respect for tradition and family.

THE JOHN MACDERMID HOUSE 1868

Elderslie Township   Concession 9   Lot15

This is the oldest stone house in Elderslie Township. It is situated on a hillside, framed by mature trees, and accompanied by fine farm buildings. The whole farmscape is one of great charm. As was usually the case, the fieldstone for the house was collected on the property.

The present owner's mother has written in *The Bruce County Historical Societies Yearbook – 1969* that, "The beams that form the foundation are twelve inches in diameter while the pine boards that were used in the wainscotting were eighteen inches across. The lime for the plaster used in the house was made in a lime-kiln on the farm where the limestone from the fields was burned. The lime-kiln was uncovered in 1967 when an area was being levelled to erect a pole barn."

The property has been owned by a succession of John MacDermids. The original John MacDermid (1855-1917) came from Islay, an island in the Inner Hebrides, off the south-west coast of Scotland. He had travelled together with his brothers and sisters to Upper Canada after the sudden death of their father in 1848. They came to Duntroon, near Collingwood, to stay with an uncle. Later, John MacDermid married Margaret Campbell (1833-1894) from Boston Mills and here in Elderslie Township they developed their beautiful farm and raised a family. Successive owners were John A., John S., and now John R. MacDermid.

THE GEORGE BROCKIE HOUSE   C.1867

Greenock Township   Concession A Part Lot 44

George Brockie, born in 1828 in Scotland, was one of the earliest settlers in Greenock Township. He came to Bruce County in 1854 and received the Patent from the Crown for his 140 acres in 1865. He is described in the H. Belden & Co.'s 1880 *Bruce County Atlas* as a farmer and general stock breeder and as a councilman.

The Brockie house was used as a granary for twenty years and was home to a large colony of raccoons until 1975 when a new owner began its restoration. The present owners are engaged in restoration of the outbuildings and of the land itself. This is a story oft-repeated in our region. Valuable examples of historic domestic architecture and of whole historic farmsteads have been saved from ruin by urbanites who have the time and resources to see to their rehabilitation.

The austere setting of the house contributes to its appeal. It is a lonely stone cottage situated among empty miles of rolling hills. Its appeal also lies in its proportions, which are right in every respect. The front gable is large enough to house a generous pointed-arch window. The remainder of the windows are large and well-placed, especially the front windows which are placed closer than usual to the door in order to contribute to the "lift" of the centre gable. The fieldstone masonry is almost Minoan in magnitude. The technical term for such stonework is "Cyclopean". George Brockie left us a legacy of grace and beauty when he planned and built his pioneer home over 130 years ago.

The Henry Cargill House   c.1888

Greenock Township   Village of Cargill

The illustrious Henry Cargill (1838-1903) was the son of Irish parents from County Antrim. He was born in Halton County and came with his wife, Margaret Davidson, to Greenock Township in Bruce County in 1879. As a public spirited and immensely capable citizen he acted as postmaster in his village from 1880 to 1887, reeve from 1885 to 1887 and Member of Parliament for East Bruce from 1887 until his death in 1903. His children were Wellington David, Carrie, Margaret and Henrietta.

The village of Cargill, located on the banks of the Teeswater River, was originally called Yokassippi, a corruption of the indigenous Indian word meaning "the drowned lands river". This referred to what is known today as the Greenock or the "Great Swamp". Before 1872 it consisted of 150,000 acres of forested wetland. Today it comprises about 20,000 acres or 250 square miles – about one-third of the area of the township. It is drained by creeks, lakes and rivers. One of the unique, natural areas of Ontario, much of the swamp is now managed by the Saugeen Valley Conservation Authority.

In early times the swamp was the site of tall stands of virgin white pine, soft maple, elm, cedar, beech, hemlock, ash and yellow birch. All but the pine have regenerated over the years. Thickets of willow, dogwoods and blue beech still make up the understorey. Delicate plants such as orchids, Indian pipe and pitcher plants thrive here as do deer, wild fowl, muskrat, raccoon, fox, weasel and squirrel.

Cargill's holdings amounted to 12,000 acres from which he harvested 5,000,000 board feet of white pine each year for twenty-five years. The trees were felled in the frozen winter months using cross-cut saws. Corduroy roads were built over the soft spots of the swamp enabling men to get about. The oxen were fitted with special shoes so they would not sink into the swamp. A canal of several miles was dug by hand. It filled with water in the spring and the logs were floated along its length until they reached the Teeswater River and then down the river to Cargill. In the village, Henry Cargill opened a sawmill, a steam planing mill, a shingle mill, grist and woollen mills, and a foundry.

Cargill was also a farmer and livestock breeder. He imported 300 head of registered shorthorn cattle from Scotland and raised Clydesdale horses, sheep and swine.

This house, aptly named *The White House*, is the only Cargill family home to survive. (A later and much grander red brick house built across the road and referred to as *The Red House* was destroyed by fire in 1919.) The style, rarely seen in this region, is known as the "stick style". The rectilinear windows and the

structure itself are outlined by boards or sticks painted in starkly contrasting colour to the body of the house. Add a few carefully chosen curving lines and a large verandah surmounted by a wrought iron grill and the result is a house which easily earns the description – picturesque. Fortunately for us, the present owners, Andy and Cathy Cormack, have taken great trouble to restore the house to its former glory.

THE PINKERTON/CONNELL HOUSE   c.1854

Greenock Township   Village of Pinkerton

"The small white clapboard house on Pinkerton's main street contains within its structure, the oldest building in the village." So writes James Connell in *Greenock Township History 1856-1981*.

David Pinkerton(1799-1874), the founder of the village, arrived in 1854. He was the son of James Pinkerton, who came from Ireland to Canada with his family in the 1820s. David and his wife, Mary Ann, eventually owned 1200 acres which they registered in the names of their sons James, Matthew, Thomas, Henry, John and Joseph. Father and sons built a dam, sawmill, grist mill, carding mill, hotel and several houses in this pleasant village on the Teeswater River.

James Connell tells us that, "A log cabin, approximately sixteen by twenty-four feet was erected as David Pinkerton's first residence and still survives. When the log cabin was no longer needed by the Pinkerton family in the 1860s it was used as a meeting hall for the local Grange. The Grange was a farmers' group dedicated to improving farming techniques and lifestyle. . . . When David Pinkerton died his son Thomas was by then a prosperous mill owner. Thomas added a frame building to the front of the old cabin, with two downstairs rooms and an attic. . . . The clapboard and timbers were cut in the first sawmill, as can be seen from the *up & down* saw marks.

"The resulting house was large enough to make a comfortable family home and Thomas Pinkerton gave the deed of the property to Mrs. McCormack for as long as she needed it. No money changed hands, and a verbal agreement was made, that when she or her descendants were finished with the house, it would be returned to the Pinkerton family.

"Mrs. McCormack . . . lived the rest of her life in the house, working out as a practical nurse and doing what she could to make ends meet . . . . Mrs. McCormack's step-daughter, Jennie, became the next occupier of the old house. She had retired from service as a housemaid in the United States and came home to live with her aged stepmother. Jennie died in 1957 at the age of 95, and at this time the old promise was recalled. She willed the old house to Gordon Pinkerton who sold it two years later to his sister Aileen Connell, mother of the present owner."

James Connell clearly remembers as a child, hearing Jennie McCormack say that when she died, she would be "looking down" to make sure nothing happened to her old house. He says a few things have happened to make him wonder about this. In 1979 a very large tree in the yard fell unexpectedly, in such a

way that the house and shed were untouched. On another occasion in 1983, the old Pinkerton Hotel, which was located only a few feet south, caught fire. It had a large television aerial mast which began to fall directly toward the old house. In mid air it suddenly twisted and bent in the middle, so that it missed the house. The fire destroyed the hotel but the house was undamaged. James Connell's uncle, Everett Pinkerton, who saw both incidents, was convinced that an unseen hand had intervened in each case. The Connells have also noticed that visitors to the house have often commented on a feeling of well-being while there. So, whether or not there is a ghost, they do at least suspect there is a "benign presence".

THE JAMES DONNELLY HOUSE   c.1876

Greenock Township   Concession 12   Lot 7

James Donnelly and his brother Patrick came to Greenock Township about 1852 from Wexford County, Ireland. Soon they had saved enough money to send for their widowed mother and six younger brothers and sisters. The Donnellys proceeded to populate the area around Pinkerton, Chepstow and Cargill. James married Ellen Desmond of Kingsbridge in 1858 and they built this fieldstone cottage about eighteen years later. They raised eight children and lived to celebrate their golden wedding anniversary. In 1895 they retired to a smaller house in Kingsbridge and their son, James II and his bride, Julia McNab, moved into this structure, a prime example of Ontario fieldstone domestic architecture.

The stones in the front elevation have been carefully chosen for variety in colour and size, and laid in a lively pattern. No two stones of the same colour abut each other. Enormous stones anchor the front corners of the house, roughly resembling quoins. The side and rear walls are composed of smaller fieldstones. Dressed stone voussoirs surmount the windows. The simple plan of a one-and-a-half storey rectangular house with a centre gable is so familiar to Ontarians that we are apt to overlook some of the most charming examples – such as this one.

The Old Convent c.1875
Greenock Township   Village of Chepstow

An early settler at Chepstow, Oliver Coumans, has written (*Greenock Township History 1856-1981*) that the village was founded in 1852 when "John and Bridget Phelan, his older brother Dennis, and their daughter Mary, floated down the Yokassippi (Teeswater) River in a large canoe hollowed out of a pine log. Here they spent the night under a huge hemlock tree. In the morning they found a rude bark shanty that the surveyors had used and this became their home until they had their log house built."

In 1926 the brick house pictured here became a convent for teaching sisters. It is one part of a complex of three buildings in the lovely village of Chepstow. The other two are the Mary Immaculate Roman Catholic church and the rectory. The convent house was built by Lawrence Hartleib in about 1875. The material is the usual buff brick. However the master mason has added important details such as corbelling at the tops of the walls and solid brick quoining at the corners of the building. The round vent in the front gable, roof brackets and bargeboard also add interest to this somewhat stolid, static composition.

THE ANDREW THOMPSON HOUSE 1878

Huron Township   Concession 7   Lot 36

John Thompson, a shoemaker, was born in Fermanagh County, Ireland in 1813. It is not known exactly when he came to Canada but he was in Toronto during the 1837 Rebellion where he joined the "Regulars". In 1853, he and his wife Elizabeth Wilson moved to Huron Township, arriving by boat via Goderich. The family, parents and six children ages two to twelve, lived in a log shanty. As was usually the case, the lot was Patented by the Crown much later, in 1871. Andrew bought the farm from his father in 1877.

Andrew married Jane in 1878, the year their fashionable Second Empire style house was built. According to the family history, the house cost $1800, a fortune in those days. The sixth generation of the Thompson family is still in residence.

This is a "grand" house in a high style usually associated with urban domestic architecture. The Second Empire style originated in Paris at the time of the rebuilding of the centre of that great city – the 1840s to the 1870s. The style is easily recognized by the curving lines of the mansard roof which allows for the storey under the roof to be as large as possible. This example is graced by front and side wooden bay windows (these could be bought as kits), decorative brackets linking the prominent cornice to the eaves, and detailed dormer windows. The brickwork also deserves mention. Solid raised quoins mark the corners of the house and the tops of the walls, which are further marked by a row of diagonally-laid brick.

Andrew and Jane Thompson's vision of a suitable home for their family has resulted in a graceful architectural legacy for the community.

The McDonald/Martyn House   c.1885

Huron Township   15 Tain Street, Ripley

This L-shaped house is built of fieldstone of many hues. It presents a picture of stability and prosperity so typical of the houses of Grey and Bruce counties. The gables are decorated with bargeboard painted in mellow colours which reflect the tonal values of the stone. And, at some time in the past, a pretty frame garage and a harmonious verandah have been added to the house. The comeliness of the building is complemented by its location on a large lot with mature trees on a quiet, dignified street.

     Archibald McDonald was born in 1846, the son of Alexander McDonald (1813-1885), who had come to Canada from the Isle of Skye, Scotland. When Alexander arrived in Canada he met and married Marjorie Christian Campbell of Carillon, Quebec. Then, in 1855, the family migrated to Bruce County. In 1871 Archibald McDonald married Elizabeth McAsh of Varna (south of Goderich). They farmed for a time and then moved to Ripley where a partnership was formed with John Humberstone in a general store business.

     The Angus Martyns lived here from 1895 until 1920. Angus (1856-1925) was the son of Donald Martyn of the Lewis Settlement, a large group of pioneers who came to Huron Township in 1852 after their eviction from the Isle of Lewis in 1851. (See description of the event on page 78.) Angus served as clerk of the township and conducted a business as notary public and conveyancer which he established in Ripley in 1889.

THE BUCKINGHAM/MACKAY HOUSE   C.1880

Huron Township   Concession 10 Lot 18

Thomas Buckingham, whose settlement in Huron Township can be traced to 1867, received the Crown Patent for this property in 1869. His impressive stone house was probably built sometime between 1875 and 1885. A son, Richard, (1846-1936) continued working the family farm with his wife Phoebe after his father's death. Sometime after she died in 1891 he married Catherine Harrison (1867-1963) and they moved to Ripley in 1901.

Neil MacKay bought the Buckingham property in 1903 when he and Sadie MacElhanney were married. He was the sixth child of Kenneth and Annie MacKay, a Gaelic speaking family from the Isle of Lewis in the Scottish Hebrides who occupied the farm next door. MacKay descendants continued to occupy this property until 1982.

The MacKays were one of 109 families who had emigrated together from the Isle of Lewis to Huron Township. They established what became known as the "Lewis Settlement". In the Hebrides they had been sailors, fishermen and shepherds existing on a diet of fish and potatoes. They were totally unfitted to be settlers in a country of solid bush which had to be cleared to make way for farming. Nevertheless, they were hardy and determined and eventually made good in their new lives.

The story of their coming to Canada is one of true grit.

Sir James Matheson had made his fortune in the opium trade in India. On his return home to Britain he secured a title, married a fashionable wife, and in 1844 paid £190,000 for the Isle of Lewis. His efforts to develop a trade in peat and agriculture ended in failure and he decided to evict his tenants from their croftings. He did provide them with funds for their passage to the new world and offered to purchase their horses, cattle and sheep. In May 1851, two hundred families left from Stornaway on three ships. One ship turned back but the *Marie Blanche* and the *Princess Alice* made the journey of nine weeks and four days. It was one of terrible hardship. Fortunately for all aboard, the men from Lewis were experienced sailors and were able to assist the ships' crews during severe storms. The ships landed in Quebec and their passengers proceeded together to Toronto, then Galt, Goderich, and finally Huron township.

The story is told ("*Families and Farms of Huron with its Hub – Ripley*") of the boat bringing the pioneers from Goderich nearing the shore at Kincardine. The women became frightened and cried that, "in such a heathen place there would be no word of God preached". But as they neared the shore, out over the water from an open air service held upon a hill came voices singing their beloved Psalms. They lost their fear and felt God was still with them.

The house has been scrupulously rehabilitated and a new verandah and upper balcony have been added. The fieldstone has been mortared to suggest squared cut stone, the edges have been darkened and fresh white lines imprinted between the stones. Even the segmental brick window heads have been outlined in white. The effect is dramatic – especially in a snowy landscape.

"Bernhardt" The Daniel Smith House c.1885

Huron Township   1 Jessie Street, Ripley

Daniel Fisher Smith (1852-1901) was the son of Jesse and Catharine Smith of Wallace Township, Perth County. He graduated in medicine from McGill University, came to Ripley in 1878 and practiced until 1894. A large part of the village was built on the twenty-five acres he acquired when he arrived. He named three of the streets – Jesse, after his father, McGill, after his alma mater and Gladstone after the British Prime Minister. And he named his house *Bernhardt* after the great actress, Sarah Bernhardt, who was touring North America at the time

Smith married Margaret Alexandrina McQueen, daughter of a Presbyterian clergyman, and they had three children. Tragically, she died in 1888 at only twenty-seven years of age. His second wife was Maria Walker who bore him two sons. Smith died prematurely of pneumonia in 1901 and his widow and family went west. The property was sold to Dr. Donald A. McCrimmon. J. B. Martyn, a merchant and the first reeve of Ripley, bought the property in 1918 and it remains in the Martyn family to this day.

As was the custom, the doctor's office was located in his home – in this case, at the rear of the house in a two-storey annex. The enterprising Dr. Smith also rebuilt the village drugstore after a fire, named it the Bruce Medical Hall and established a second office there.

The house is built of buff brick three layers deep. The only approach is to the side of the building because Smith was never granted permission by the village council to open his property to the main street – the direction in which he built his house.

Fortunately, it fully retains its original character. The verticality of the building is best seen from the front elevation. It is two-and-a-half storeys in height and has a steeply pitched roof. The front-facing gable is beautifully decorated with elegant, scalloped bargeboard. The enclosed verandah, which off-sets the height of the building, is an early addition.

The Doll House   c.1860 (tower c.1890)
Kincardine   860 Huron Terrace

This picturesque house has some of the hallmarks of the style known as Carpenter Gothic, so-named because the skills of the carpenter or woodworker are in full evidence. The bargeboard and kingpin in the north part of the building and diamond decoration in wood in the tower attest to the builder's talent and ability.

The house is an eclectic combination of 1860s Gothic Revival and 1890s Stick Style (the latter as seen in the tower). By what means this came about is not known. However, there is no doubt that the house emanates a certain charm which is reinforced by its authentic building materials, such as cedar roof shingles and shiplap exterior walls.

It is thought that the Rev. Walter Inglis had his house built soon after he bought the property in 1859. Inglis had been the superintendent of education for the western district of Bruce county from 1859 until 1861. He had also held Presbyterian services in North Kinloss and Riversdale from 1857. In 1859 Inglis was called to West Church in Kincardine, a United Presbyterian congregation, where he served for ten years.

A Francis Walker House   c.1855

Kincardine   217 Harbour Street

The Regency cottage was an early building type in Upper Canada favoured by retired military officers and other members of the upper class who had the intention and the means to bring old world architectural sensibilities to the new world. Although they appear diminutive, these charming one-storey houses were often built with full basements to accommodate kitchen, laundry, storage rooms and servants' quarters. The main floor was designed with a broad centre hall with two large rooms on either side – the dining room, parlour and two bedrooms. Ceilings were high and wood mouldings were elegant.

The exterior of the Regency cottage featured a truncated, hipped roof – in this case topped with an iron crest of great charm. Entrances are flanked by a transom and sidelights and windows are large and usually glazed in a six-panes over six-panes pattern. This porch is a later addition.

Francis "Paddy" Walker is listed in early directories as a "gentleman", an interesting euphemism used by early census-takers to mean a settler with cash resources. Born in 1801 in Ireland, Walker came to Kincardine in 1850 by travelling north from Goderich on the ice in a cutter. With him were his wife, Jane, and seven sons. Later that year he lost his ship, *The Mud Turtle*, on the rocks off Point Clark. The cargo was lost but the crew survived.

He built a major hotel in Kincardine which he named Walker House. It still stands today despite a fire in 1994. Paddy Walker is noted by town historians as the man who was responsible for altering the course of the Penetangore River to bring it closer to his hotel door. He was a colourful character whose ability to use salty language was unparalleled.

"ARDLOCH" THE SUMMER HOME OF
SIR ALEXANDER MACKENZIE   C.1900
Kincardine   219 Lambton Street

This house was built for Wintringham Cliften Luscombe (1843-1909), a practicing lawyer in Kincardine. But ever since Kincardine's most famous native son bought the house in 1928 as his summer retirement home, and gave it the name *Ardloch*, the house has been associated with Sir Alexander Mackenzie. The Royal Canadian Legion is the present owner.

In 1980, Kincardine newspaperman, Robert Stewart, wrote a full account of the life of Mackenzie for the booklet, *Kincardine – Glimpses of the Past*. The following is drawn from that article.

Alexander Mackenzie's birth in 1860 in Kincardine, Ontario did not auger a future as the town's most famous son. He was born, one of ten children, to Donald Mackenzie, a local blacksmith, and his wife. When he was seventeen Alexander left Kincardine to article as a lawyer in the Toronto firm of Blake, Lash & Cassels. While in his thirties and a junior member of the firm he was chosen to represent the interests of Sir William Mackenzie (no relation) in the Brazilian Traction Co. of South America.

In 1899 mule-driven tramways moved through the streets of Sao Paulo, Brazil. They were owned by a Brazilian, Americo de Campos and an Italian from Montreal, Francisco Gualco. Gualco realized the potential of electrifying the tramways and raised money in Toronto from Sir William Mackenzie for the purpose. The deal was handled by Blake, Lash & Cassels and thus entered Alexander Mackenzie into Brazilian affairs. He was made vice-president of the company and, although he was commissioned to stay in Brazil only six months, he stayed for thirty years and within fifteen years became the president of Brazilian Traction – now known as Brascan Corporation.

By the time of Mackenzie's death in 1943, the Brazilian Traction, Light & Power Co. Ltd. was the world's largest utility and Brazil's largest single corporation.

Mackenzie married Mabel Blake, daughter of the Honorable Samuel Hume Blake of Toronto in

1908 and they made their home in Brazil. He was knighted in 1919 for his work in Brazil and for his contribution to the war effort. He had been active in the Red Cross and financed a military hospital at Kingston Hill, Surrey, England.

In 1938 Mackenzie made *Ardloch* in Kincardine his home base. The people of Kincardine nicknamed him "The Light" for obvious reasons. He loved to walk his dogs along the beach and was a benefactor to the town. He gave a shoreline park to the town in memory of his friend, James McPherson. He built lawn bowling and tennis grounds, a manse for the Presbyterian church and supported the local hospital. He died childless and most of his fortune went to charity anonymously.

THE JOHN SCOUGALL HOUSE   C.1886

Kincardine   750 Princes Street

There is a remarkable consistency of bargeboard design in Kincardine. The example in this house closely resembles that of the Doll House, (page 83) and the Jonas Vanstone House (page 101), very likely because it was supplied by a local factory. Graceful three-dimensional curves are counterpoised with rick-rack curves – all flowing into a crocket-like finial which marks the peak of the gable.

The basic style of the house is the so-called Regency Cottage. In this case the classicism of Regency has been modified by the large gable with its shapely gothic tracery.

John Scougall was born in England and came to Kincardine in 1874. In 1875 he was appointed town clerk and up until the time of his death (1922) filled this position in a manner that gained him the reputation of being one of the best municipal officers in Ontario. He was fond of the outdoor life and kept himself in vigorous condition by exercise. When informed of his death one citizen said, "He never did a shabby thing in his life".

Scougall was a photographer of note and has left us hundreds of glass plate negatives, taken between about 1895 and 1914, depicting the life and times of Kincardine. Some of these valuable photographs have been reproduced in this volume. He has provided us with a rare opportunity to compare the buildings of Kincardine as they were soon after they were erected with their present condition one hundred or so years later. In some cases his photographs provide the only evidence we have of remarkable buildings which have been demolished.

"LYNDEN HALL" c.1870
Kincardine   513 Kincardine Ave.

Here is another Second Empire style house built by A. J. Evans, the noted Kincardine architect and builder. Evan's trademark details are here: half dormers built into the eaves of the mansard roof, dentillated cornice, long windows and generous entrance. What is missing today from the structure can be seen in the vintage photo – a three-sided, awning-roofed verandah with an upper balcony, and a glazed external entry. The latter was a practical appendage to a house in our cold, northern climate.
We know from the Belden 1880 *Bruce County Atlas* that W. H. Carpenter, for whom the house was built, was a partner in the Carpenter & McCallum Combined Steam & Water Mill, built on the site of Kincardine's first mill.

Ethel M. Johnstone has written a delightful family memoir, now in the possession of the Bruce County Archives, in which she tells of her father buying the Carpenter house in about 1895 when she was seventeen years old. At that time it had been vacant for more than seven years and was considered by the local folk to be haunted by the deceased former lady of the house. Strong men whipped their horses past the place and even the canny Scots of the district "thought Father was daft and we were of the same opinion".

Johnstone writes, "The story was that the former owner, a wealthy race horse man who was away from home most of the time, had been cruel and unfaithful to his wife and she had died of a broken heart. It had been on the market all these years and the price had finally come down to a quarter of the value of the property. Dad had no fear of ghosts and he dearly loved a bargain. We sold our farm and moved in with mixed feelings. It had this awful ghost, we were leaving all our old and true friends but we would be near Kincardine, a city!"

There is no record of a subsequent "ghostly" appearance.

Photo courtesy of the Bruce County Museum and Archives, Scougall Collection.

MALCOLM PLACE   C.1875
Kincardine   255 Durham Street

This Italianate house is one of the architectural gems of Bruce County. It was likely designed by an American architect for its New York City owner, Levi Rightmeyer (1822-1895). He came to know Kincardine because he had sent his wife, Isabel Scott, there to recover her health away from the polluted air of New York city. She had several brothers resident in Kincardine. Eventually, he sold his publishing business in New York and came to Kincardine to try his luck in the salt mining business.

He built his salt plant at huge cost in the early 1870s. The wells from which the brine was extracted were sunk almost 1000 feet deep. Huge evaporating pans made of boiler iron lined with stone were heated by live steam pipes passing through the brine. Fuel, in the early mines, was cordwood purchased from farmers clearing their land. The precipitated salt was removed by an endless chain rake and deposited in bins.

Rightmeyer's plan was to ship salt in bulk to Chicago but he was foiled in this attempt by the American government which passed a tariff against Canadian salt. His Canadian salt trade was too small to be profitable and he lost the best part of his fortune. He persisted in the salt mining business until about 1894 when he sold his house and left Kincardine.

Madame Josephine Gualco bought the property in 1905. She was the wealthy widow of Sir Alexander Mackenzie's colleague in Brazilian Traction, Francisco Gualco.

In 1920 the building became the home of James Malcolm (1889-1935), Liberal MP for North Bruce 1921-1930, Minister of Trade and Commerce 1926-1930, and chairman of the Andrew Malcolm Furniture Co. His father, Andrew, had been a longtime partner in the furniture manufacturing business with fellow Scot, John Watson. The company was taken over by Andrew Malcolm in 1894 at the time of Watson's death. Furniture making was the major industry in Kincardine for over a century. Many Kincardine boys left school at the end of grade eight to apprentice in two factories, the Andrew Malcolm Co. and the Coombe Furniture Co. Ltd.

During WWII the company built components for Mosquito airplanes which were used as pathfinders in bombing missions. By 1941 the company employed more than 250 workers.

The Malcolm family sold the plant to Simmons Furniture Co. in 1973. It was closed in 1976 and the empty building was consumed by fire in 1978.

The classical detailing of the exterior is of a high order, especially the carved stone lintels, pilasters and bracketted lug sills which add importance to the already large windows. Tripartite, arched windows on all four sides of the tower, relatively low pitch of all the roofs, (compare with the pitch of the roof on the Solomon Secord House – page 99) wide eaves with dominant brackets, quoins and stringcourses give the building a decidedly "Italian" look.

The Keyworth/Mitchell House c.1875

Kincardine   776 Princes Street

Norman Robertson states in his *History of the County of Bruce*, that John Keyworth came to Canada from England in 1851 and in August of that year applied to the Crown for the Mill Block in Kincardine. He went back to England to fetch his family, leaving the building of a good-sized mill in the hands of a local contractor. When he returned to Kincardine it was clear that the framing of the building had been so botched that the mill could not be completed. Keyworth gave up the idea of milling and confined himself to keeping store until his death nine years later. His family stayed on and it was his son, Richard, who was the likely builder of this house on property purchased in the name of his wife, Lucretia Keyworth, in 1871.

In 1915 James Malcolm bought the property for $3000. He sold it in 1935 to William Mitchell for $6275.

An article in the Financial Post, October 6, 1945 and reprinted in *Kincardine – 1848-1984*, tells the story of William Mitchell's, Circle Bar Knitting Company in Kincardine.

"Back in the early days of the last war a small-town Ontario merchant saw his potential customers gradually drifting to jobs in the big cities. Instead of closing up and following he decided to do something that would reverse the trend.

"He was convinced that there were plenty of opportunities for himself and his fellow citizens right at home, and he invested his $15,000 of savings in a new employment-providing venture to prove it.

"That was the beginning of William Mitchell's, Circle Bar Knitting Co., a concern which now (1945) ships its hosiery and other products all over Canada. His mills in Owen Sound, Listowel and Kincardine employed nearly 500 people.

"In 1915 he owned a general store in Kincardine and business was good. The town's main industries then were furniture factories, a pork-packing plant and a salt block, all of which employed only male help. Several families with grown daughters moved to Hamilton and Toronto where the girls could find work, and Mr. Mitchell began to notice that it hurt his store business.

"The only answer was to provide some sort of work for women, so that they and their families could remain in town. Mr. Mitchell knew a lot of people in the knitting business – he bought their products for his store – and a small knitting mill sounded like the answer."

William Mitchell's house is designed in the French Second Empire style so popular in Kincardine. Dormers in the slate mansard roof light the attic. The centre tower, which accommodates the main entrance is topped by its own mansard roof. Brick quoins define the corners of the house and bay windows add interest to the front façade.

95

THE MCKENDRICK/WATSON HOUSE   C.1900

Kincardine   791 Princes Street

This imposing house embodies the concept of eclecticism in architectural design. The use of a mixture of styles in one building can be convincing in the hands of a confident designer. In this case, design elements from different eras are well integrated into the whole. Queen Anne Revival multiple wall planes and roof intersections and suggestion of a tower, Edwardian pediment over the porch entry, Richardsonian half-round parlour window with a heavy stone lintel, and Arts & Crafts window glazing, all combine pleasingly in this large house.

George McKendrick, commissioner and druggist bought the property in 1895 and soon after built this family home.

In 1910 it was sold for $3,275 to James Watson, the owner in 1858 of the first furniture-making shop in Kincardine. The Watson family lived here for over fifty years. It is interesting to note that in the early years Watson used horse-power to drive his machinery. Andrew Malcolm joined John Watson in 1894 and their company was known for thirty-five years as Watson & Malcolm. After the death of its founders it became the nationally known Andrew Malcolm Furniture company.

PHOTO COURTESY OF THE BRUCE COUNTY MUSEUM AND ARCHIVES, SCOUGALL COLLECTION.

THE SOLOMON SECORD HOUSE   C.1870

Kincardine   276 Durham Street

Dr. Solomon Secord came to Bruce County in the late 1850s, practiced medicine briefly in Walkerton and then came to Kincardine. His advertisement in the 1867 Bruce County Directory reads, "S.S. Secord, M.D. Physician, Surgeon, Accoucheur. Coroner for the County of Bruce. Residence and Office Lambton Street, Kincardine." Soon after he moved his residence and office to this house on Durham Street.

Dr. Secord married Elvira Crable and they had three children. Mrs. Secord was in the habit of preparing more food than the family needed because she knew Solomon was likely to bring visitors home at mealtime. He had a generous heart and did not press his patients for payment. He loved children, a passion that was returned manyfold. They were often seen climbing into his buggy when he made his rounds.

Secord's early history is stranger than fiction. He was an outspoken abolitionist who travelled from Kincardine to Georgia where he found himself enmeshed in the American Civil War. Although he was opposed to slavery he was sympathetic to the political aims of the American south and served as a medical officer in the Confederate army for the duration. One account of his life (*Kincardine – Glimpses of the Past*) claims that he was arrested because of his anti-slavery views and, but for a daring rescue by his friends, was almost hanged after a rigged trial. When he rejoined the army of the South in 1863 at Fort McHenry near Baltimore, he was captured by Northern forces and placed in a prison camp from which he and several others escaped. He continued to serve in the war as supervisor of hospitals with the rank of Surgeon-General.

Journalist Colonel Hugh Clarke wrote in an obituary, "Secord loved the open air, the fields and flowers and if he had any hobby it was gardening . . . Physically he was a marvel of toughness and endurance . . . Every old citizen has a story to tell of his courage, his endurance, his generosity, his marvellous power as a diagnostician, his wonderful skill as a physician. He will surely be missed in this community that knew him for fifty years as a lover of justice, a hater of sham, a simple, natural, unaffected man who did more good than this world will ever know."

A monument to his memory was erected beside the library, the cost of which was paid by his friends – people from the town, the county and all over North America.

You see in this photograph the only remaining authentic façades of his house and office. Gothic Revival in style, it is distinguished by a steeply pitched roof punctuated by gothic dormers. Brick labels surmount the tall, narrow windows. Two gables are still lined with the original, graceful bargeboard.

THE JOHN MCLEOD HOUSE C.1880

Kincardine   433 Broadway

The centre frontispiece of this house, which provides for a vestibule inside the entrance, also extends above the roof to form a low tower. This tower with its arcade of double, round-headed windows and Italianate roofline gives the austere house its character. It is built of brick, painted white, with contrasting black window shutters.

John McLeod was born in 1828 in Cape Breton. He came to Kincardine about 1867 when he bought this property. It remained in the family until 1919 when his widow, Elizabeth, sold the house and property for $3,000. He was a main street merchant dealing in dry goods, groceries, hardware, clothing and boots and shoes.

The Jonas Vanstone House   c.1876

Kincardine   267 Lambton Street

The better examples of the Gothic Revival style of domestic architecture in Ontario always include an ample centre gable in a gable-ends roof configuration. In addition, the window within that centre gable often reflects the Gothic tradition of the pointed arch, or in this case, the inflected or ogee arch. This house qualifies as an excellent example of Ontario Gothic on both counts. Other gothic elements present are the roof finials and eye-catching bargeboard. A later verandah has been added, half of which is glazed. The verandah poses an interesting contrast between the gothic gable of the house and the classical porch pediment.

Jonas Vanstone, one of five sons of Richard Vanstone, came with his father and brothers to Bruce County from England in 1855. He and his brother Josiah are listed in various directories as builders or contractors. Jonas bought this property in 1870 and his house provides a convincing demonstration of his abilities as a builder.

The A.J. Evans House   c.1875

Kincardine   689 Princes Street

Abraham Joseph Evans (1839-1912) left his mark on the town of Kincardine in a way rarely found in small-town Ontario. He built houses of distinction which, fortunately, still stand today as a testament to his talent for grace and restraint in architectural design.

His own house, pictured here, is a miniature French chateau. It is built in the style he preferred – French Second Empire. Its proportions are perfect, its ornamentation delicate, controlled. It has been meticulously maintained and remains a favourite among the houses of Bruce County.

The tower with its gracefully curved mansard roof is the focal point of this decorous lady. Its height, four well-shaped dormers, wrought iron crest and decorative brickwork call attention to the house. The dormers in the main roof are topped with classical pediments. A generous entrance, a pleasant bay window and a refined verandah and upper balcony complete the portrait.

A. J. Evans was an architect and builder from Swansea, South Wales who came to Bruce County in 1861. The 1871 Bruce County census modestly lists him as an English carpenter. Lynden Hall, another of his houses is pictured in this volume, page 90.

THE VANSTONE HOUSE   c. 1875

Kincardine   1083 Queen Street

Richard Vanstone, listed as "gentleman" in various early directories, was born in England in 1801. He came to Bruce County in 1855 with sons, Jonas, Joseph, Josiah, J.J. and Richard Jr. His sons were builders and stone cutters – well positioned to construct the buildings of a new village. Jonas, Josiah and Richard Jr. operated a large planing mill and sash and door factory on Lambton Street. Joseph and J.J. are variously listed as stone cutters and owners of a marble works on Queen Street.

A son, Joseph Vanstone, bought half an acre from George Barry in 1873 and over the next nine years took out mortgages totalling $16,000 with which to build this significant house.

Ralph Greenhill, Ken Macpherson and Douglas Richardson in their book, *Ontario Towns*, wrote, "The more refined stonework marks this house as an urban example of the familiar, later 19th century house. A narrow, projecting centre with a shallow gable – or pediment – but deep eaves on a hipped-roofed block are the distinguishing features of the type. The paired brackets of especially complex form under the eaves suggest a date in the 1870s for this example. In its general effect, the rich (and strangely assorted) treatment of the stone trim recalls the opulence of some Italianate commercial buildings of the previous decade."

The bizarre belvedere is a replacement of the original equally bizarre belvedere shown in the vintage photograph.

PHOTO COURTESY OF THE "KINCARDINE 1848-1984"

Kincardine Township

The Cole/Glass House c.1873
Kincardine Township   Part Lot 18 Concession 2 SDR (South of the Durham Road)

This fifty acre property lies one concession south of the settlement trail known as the Durham Road. James Cole, born in 1830 and his wife Mary, born in 1831, came here with their three-year old daughter Rosie, in 1854. Cole received the Crown Patent for his property in 1869 and took out mortgages amounting to $1,600 in the early 1870s. The house was built then or shortly after by the next owner of the property, Irvin Glass, who acquired it in 1874.

Glass (1828-1910) and his wife Jane Carlton (1839-1915), raised their family here and in 1905 turned the farm over to Irvin Jr. and his wife, Henrietta. Although the Glass family made their home here for fifty-seven years we know little of them.

We can, however, describe the next family to live here. Ernest Owen (1890-1980) came to Canada in about 1910 from Oldham, England. He and his wife Henrietta (1895-1985) and their four children developed a market garden business – supplying local retailers with raspberries, strawberries, potatoes and other garden produce until 1970.

One of the prettiest Gothic Revival houses in the south of Bruce County this example, although reclad with metal sheeting, retains its significant characteristics. These include the flattened-arch windows with conforming shutters and the pedimented porch at the front door which echoes the lines of the centre gable. The gable itself is lined with trefoil bargeboard and encloses a gothic window, again with conforming shutters. This house without the echoing shutters would lose much of its distinction.

The Hurdon/McKenzie House c.1875

Kincardine Township   Lots 5 & 6 Concession 1 SDR (South of the Durham Road)

William Hurdon, a grain buyer and MP for Bruce, purchased the property in 1875 and built this fifteen-room house. At one time it had a large verandah and a belvedere of twelve windows reached by a circular staircase of nine steps from the attic. It was a grand house with five fireplaces, two bathrooms and a front hall eight feet wide.

The design of the house is classically inspired. It is a cube with strictly symmetrical openings, dentil mouldings in the cornice and a decorated frieze. Added to this basic design is an advancing bay with gothic window glazing and a massive gothic triple arch entrance. This house is a fine example of the free and easy mixing of architectural styles in the Victorian era to achieve variation and appeal in design.

In 1879 Donald McKenzie bought the farm, removed the back portion and built more modern servants' quarters. As many as twenty-four people lived and worked here at the turn of the century when McKenzie's son, Kenneth, and his wife, Jaffray, were running the farm. When Delco was invented for power, its first use in Kincardine Township was at the McKenzie farm. It produced electricity for lighting, pumping water, separating cream and grinding feed.

Work began on the McKenzie farm at 6 am. Ten or twelve cows were milked by machine and the milk was separated. A big windmill pumped water and did the chopping. Kenneth kept about seventy cattle, a dozen horses, pigs and poultry and ran modern machinery of every kind. Jaffray had two housekeepers, both excellent cooks.

On Saturday night field work stopped at five o'clock and all chores were done up before supper. After the meal the hired men went up to Kenneth's smoking room where he made out their cheques and gave them Sunday off.

Lion's Head

THE EVERATT HOUSE C.1890
Lion's Head   8 Everatt Street

One of the first settlers in the Lion's Head area of the Bruce Peninsula was John Everatt who arrived about 1875. He and his wife, Elizabeth, are listed in an 1881 tax roll. As a farmer, he was a man of initiative, being the first in the region to grow winter wheat and to harvest it using a chopping mill he built himself. In her later years Elizabeth Everatt told local historians that crops grown on their virgin land were "wonderful!"

Their house is situated on land rising west of the main street of the village. It is an expression of a generic Ontario style of one-and-a-half storeys with a central entrance and centre gable above. The additions behind harmonize well with the house.

PHOTO COURTESY MICHAEL AND KAREN HENDERSON

The Moore/Meneray House   1883
Lion's Head   64 Main Street

Robert E. Moore, a merchant, built this frame house in 1883 for his wife and three children. It was considered the first "grand" house to be built in the village of Lion's Head. Its L plan with rear extensions was a prototypical design in Ontario in the late 19th century. The dormers which rise through the roofline, the generous windows and the overall asymmetry of the house give it a picturesque charm. Some of the framing detail of the windows has been lost in successive claddings of the house – first insulbrick and then vinyl. Moore hired an English gardener to landscape the extensive grounds including a bowling green for which underground water piping was installed.

After the Moores left the house in 1903, one of the most colourful of a succession of owners was Dr. John Sloan, son of a pioneer physician from Annan in Grey county. Walter Warder in his book, *Between You & Me and the Gatepost* wrote, "Dr. Sloan got our druggist, George Armstrong, to administer the anaesthetic, and he would scrub up and perform operations on the kitchen table and sometimes by coal oil lamps when necessity demanded it. He did at least twenty operations of this nature with only one fatality due to rupture of the appendix, having been called too late." A restless soul, Dr. Sloan soon left Lion's Head for Edmonton, then on to France during WWI, Ireland, and finally England. He was known everywhere he practiced as a brilliant surgeon.

Emary Meneray (1903-1975) bought the house in 1931 when he married Vera Hewton (1911-1986). The Menerays were mariners and fishermen on Georgian Bay. Their tugs and fishing boats were well-known to local residents. They ran the *Molly S.* (later renamed the *N. Molly M.*), the *Stocker*, the *A.G. Meneray* (built in Owen Sound in 1924), the *W. E. Meneray*, and the *Touche*. The Menerays were considered excellent sailors and as fishermen were superlative. They fished out of Wingfield Basin in the summer and Lion's Head in the autumn, catching whitefish and lake trout.

THE RICHARD TACKABERRY HOUSE   c.1890

Lion's Head   46 Main Street

This commanding fieldstone house was built by the Forbes brothers, Scottish stone masons, for Lion's Head merchant Richard Tackaberry (1845-1923) and his wife Mary Jane Bradley. Richard's father Nathaniel (1818-1874) was the first settler in Lion's Head, arriving in the late 1860s. He later went "outside", to urban areas in the south, to encourage settlement in the area. The 1871 census lists Nathaniel, 50 years, his wife Margaret, 45 years and their seven children, the oldest of whom was Richard.

The Tackaberry family had come to Canada from County Carlow in Ireland in 1847 and to the Bruce Peninsula in 1869. They played an important role in the life of the community. Richard helped build the settlement roads, was a charter member of the Orange Lodge and was the area tax collector. A brother, John, was clerk of Lion's Head for more than thirty years.

This massive two-and-a-half storey house towers over the streetscape. Its walls are thirty-three inches thick, and its steeply pitched roof carries a belvedere. Finials mark the gable peaks and the stone quoins are enormous. The verandah is a recent addition.

THE STUART/WARDER HOUSE   1887

Lion's Head   37 Main Street

Built on land originally Patented by Robert Moore, this house was erected by a Mr. McKenzie of Wiarton for farmer and lumberman, Frank Stuart and his family. Stuart is considered the "father" of Lion's Head for good reason. He laid out the village, built the first store and post office, boarded the road workers, founded the local agricultural fair and was Justice of the Peace. His barn was said to be the finest in the Peninsula.

This two-storey house was built of rough-sawn hemlock. The space between the hemlock and the inner walls was filled with grout. The exterior was then veneered with brick in two colours. It is a four-square house, a simple cube. The bow windows and projecting entrance on the main floor break up the severe exterior elevations.

Eli Warder (1851-1915) came to Canada from the Isle of Wight as an infant with his parents, Richard and Ann Warder. In 1877 he and his wife Emma Kivell (1853-1923), and their children – four year old Hannah, two year old Lily, and six month old George, migrated to the Bruce Peninsula. They landed north of Lion's Head at Whippoorwill Bay and walked through the woods to their lot at Ferndale, several miles distant. They lived in a shack already on the lot, later building a log house and covering it with clapboard. In 1902, after twenty-five years in this location, they moved to the Stuart house and farm at Lion's Head.

Their son Walter, and his son Maitland, have published valuable local histories, (*Between You and Me and the Gatepost* in 1977 and *Footloose on the Bruce* in 1994). They carried out successful farming operations, and served on many regional boards and committees.

Paisley

"THE BLACK AND WHITE HOUSE"   C.1895
Paisley   570 Queen Street North

This striking cottage was likely built to a plan from an American house pattern book. The architectural type, referred to as Stick style, was popular in the last part of the nineteenth century, particularly in the United States. The black trim on the white clapboard exterior reinforces the visual impact of the skeletal structure as well as the roof brackets and the window treatment. And, in this case, the truncated-hip roof in black anchors all these elements in place.

The Patents for the land in this part of Paisley were granted by the Crown to Robert Young and William W. Smith, both listed in the 1867 County of Bruce directory as "Gentlemen".

"MILLBANK" THE ARCHIE FISHER HOUSE 1894
Paisley   308 Mill Street

The history of this property dates back to 1857 when a settler by the name of Lyons bought it from Samuel T. Rowe and started building a dam and framing a sawmill. James Hanna continued the project by finishing the dam, cutting out the mill race and erecting a grist mill.

In 1869 Duncan Fisher bought the Hanna mills and added another dam, a sawmill and a carding & woollen mill. An 1899 advertisement for the business reads, "The woolen mill employees 11 hands in the manufacture of tweeds, blankets and fine & coarse woollens of all kinds and turns out 100 yards daily." Duncan's brother, Archie, became the owner of the A. Fisher & Son Flour Mills and advertised, "They manufacture and keep on hand for wholesale and retail, flour made from Ontario and Manitoba wheat, also all kinds of mill feed." The sawmill business advertised, "They manufacture all kinds of lumber, shingles & lath, dressed & matched ceiling, flooring, rustic & wainscoting . . . " Truly, a family empire was in the making.

Work on Archie Fisher's house began in 1891 and progressed slowly. It was finished complete with tower in 1894. B. Eric Parker wrote in his booklet, *Paths of Paisley*, "The house is spacious and distinctive and commands a beautiful view".

THE DR. PETER McLAREN HOUSE   1874
Paisley   232 Church Street

Dr. Peter McLaren, a graduate of McGill University, came to Paisley in September 1861. His practice grew quickly along with the development of the village and the surrounding farmland, particularly after the arrival of the railroad in August, 1872. He had been preceded in Paisley by Dr. Stephen Crawford, father of poet Isabella Valancy Crawford. Robert Fulford, the well-known Canadian literary critic, has described Isabella Crawford as "the grandmother figure of Canadian literature".

Dr. McLaren acted as coroner for Bruce and Huron counties, and as treasurer of the village of Paisley. He was succeeded in this impressive house by Drs. O'Neill, H. E. Gage, and Joseph Grove.

The structure presents a mellow appearance because it is built of buff brick with its wooden parts painted cream and a pale woodland green. The style is a vernacular version of the fashionable Second Empire style of architecture of the late 19th century originally associated with the court of Emperor Napoleon III of France. This example is distinguished by round-headed windows surmounted by keystone lintels. The dormer windows of the top half-floor are richly ornamented. Wide eaves are supported by decorative brackets. The mansard roof is particularly pleasing because of its exaggerated curving silhouette.

THE DAVID D. HANNA HOUSE 1866 (date stone)

Paisley 376 Victoria Street North

This lovely house has been designated a heritage property under the Ontario Heritage Act for two reasons – its architectural value and integrity, and its association with several historic figures of Paisley.

Samuel T. Rowe, born in 1819 in Cornwall, England and the original owner of this property, came here in 1851. He and Simon Orchard arrived several weeks apart on rafts made of cedar logs. They had floated down the fast-flowing Saugeen River from Walkerton. The rafts, said to have measured thirty feet by fifteen feet, carried them, their families and all their household goods. They both chose the confluence of the Saugeen and the Teeswater rivers as their landing place; Rowe on the north side of the Saugeen and Orchard on the south. They managed communication with each other by means of a dog named Danger, which carried small articles and messages back and forth!

In 1852 the government reserved land here for a village and both men were granted Patents from the Crown. The Town Plot was surveyed in 1855 and the village quickly grew as a regional centre.

In 1858 David Hanna, a lawyer, purchased this property from Samuel Rowe and in 1866 he built his house. By this time Hanna had developed a grist mill and a sawmill and built them into a profitable village industry. He also built a hotel and the famous waterwheel steamer, *The Water Witch* in which he planned to transport people and goods between Walkerton and Paisley on the Saugeen River. In 1869 Hanna sold the mill privilege to Duncan Fisher but retained his house until 1875.

The house, a picturesque example of Gothic Revival is situated just north of the mill pond dike. Mature trees and extensive grounds frame its Gothic elevations. A large bay window with Gothic tracery centres the front elevation. It is an early and congenial addition to the house. Above the bay window is a balcony, a date stone and typical Gothic style bargeboard with a drop finial in the gable. Double verandahs provide shelter for coming and going, as well as outdoor living space with a view of the garden. The house is constructed of a double layer of red brick trimmed with buff brick quoins and the steeply pitched roof is pierced by four chimneys.

Paisley, like other river valley villages in Bruce County, has the quality of that imaginary Hollywood confection called *Brigadoon*. Villages and towns such as Chesley, Chepstow, Pinkerton and Walkerton are extraordinarily pretty because of their locations beside picturesque rivers and because of the admirable 19th century houses and commercial buildings which still grace their streets.

The Claxton/McLennan House   c.1885

Paisley   287 George Street South

About 1880, John Claxton, in partnership with Samuel Ballachy, ran a general store in the village of Paisley. They advertised, "All lines of merchandise – dry goods, boots & shoes – in good quality at fair prices". No hype, no false claims, no pie in the sky. Just "good quality at fair prices". Their store building dated back to about 1854 when it was erected for the town's first settler, first merchant and first postmaster, Thomas Orchard. Claxton bought the property on which his house was built in 1880. From 1911 until 1969 the house was owned by Elizabeth and Roderick McLennan. Here they raised their children – Roderick, William, George, Jean and Annie.

It is a structure of great charm. The brickwork is of a high order. There is variety in the rooflines, an attractive bay window, wooden plank walkways and verandahs made comely by carpentry in the design-mode of the Aesthetic Period of the late nineteenth century. The situation of the house is prime. It hugs the ground in a hollow by the river. It would be impossible to find a more pleasing house of the period anywhere in the region.

Port Elgin

The Henry Hilker House   c.1865
Port Elgin   705 Goderich Street

Many of the first settlers of Port Elgin were German. One of the very first was Henry Hilker. Norman Robertson in his *History of the County of Bruce* writes, "Henry Hilker was born near Heidelburg, Germany, in 1824 . . . He came with his father to Preston in 1837. In the fall of 1852 Mr. Hilker came to Bruce. After taking up land, part of which is now in Port Elgin, he returned to Waterloo. In the following spring he brought his family with him to his bush farm. From then until his death (1900) Mr. Hilker was constantly engaged in enterprises which helped make Port Elgin all that it is today. As a member of the firm of Ruby & Hilker, merchants and grain buyers, his name became widely known throughout the county. . . Mr. Hilker held the reeveship of Saugeen for three years, and that of Port Elgin for seven years."

Hilker's solid, buff brick Georgian style house on the main street of Port Elgin is now a bar. The house has lost its crowning belvedere, its shutters and its charming striped, awning-roofed verandah – the elements which lightened the well-proportioned severity of the house. Fortunately, the handsome wrought iron fence and delicately wrought gate remain. Although the house is in the Georgian style, the builder-designer just couldn't keep himself from providing a little flat "gothic" in the centre-front roof.

Photo courtesy of the Bruce County Museum and Archives

128

THE WILLIAM H. RUBY HOUSE   c.1890

Port Elgin   543 Mill Street

Elizabeth Price has written about this building in her booklet, *Exploring the Bruce – a Driving Tour*, "The front gables, which face different directions in an interesting fashion, mount towards a central peak." Not only that, the gables are lit by Palladian windows and joined by a two-storey arcaded porch which boasts slender columns, unusual bargeboard and a lacy iron-work grill. The prominent quoins emphasize the wall intersections of differing angles and decorated pressed "stone" (cast cement) lintels overhang the large rectangular windows.

Of German descent, William Ruby (1830-1892) was born in New Jersey and migrated to Port Elgin in 1854. He and Henry Hilker founded the Ruby Hilker General Store. He became the town treasurer, a post he held for many years. Catherine (1845-1919) and William Ruby raised six children.

The James Muir House 1888 (date stone)

Port Elgin   510 Mill Street

This house is given extra interest by the design of a side entrance with portico, a handsome round-headed window to light the inner stairwell, and a two-storey square bay topped by a pedimented gable.

James Muir, born in Scotland in 1828, came to Port Elgin in 1856 with his wife, Jane Fleming. She died in 1870 leaving six young children. According to family legend, James Muir had trouble getting satisfactory housekeepers until he married Jessie Robertson in 1875.

He is listed in the 1869 Bruce County directory as a carpenter. In time he established the Excelsior Planing Mill and the Muir Furniture and Undertakers Co. He was a public spirited citizen, serving as a town councillor for several years.

The McCannel House   c.1894

Port Elgin   536 Mill Street

The McCannel family fortune came from their clothing business, the Port Elgin Men's Ready to Wear & Made to Measure. Alex McCannel (1833-1926) and Sarah (1845-1945) built their buff brick house in the prevailing Italianate style – a style which expressed their relative wealth and sophistication. It is a two-storey cube with wide overhanging eaves descending from a hipped roof, which at one time was crowned with a belvedere. The present owners claim that when the remains of two massive chimneys in the attic were removed during renovations, "the house rose!" A bay window gives variety to the wall plane at one side of the house. Single rows of dyed black bricks emphasize the roof-line, the stringcourses, and the segmental window heads.

As was the custom in this area a tail was built onto the rear of the house – in this case in brick – in order to add living space. The front entrance retains its original winning design features: panelled door, transom and sidelights, and graceful bevelled posts linked with arches to support the porch roof.

THE JESSE SHIER HOUSE   C.1875

Port Elgin   591 Elgin Street

The decorative brickwork in the gable and under the roofline in the form of corbelled brick bargeboard, together with the unusually pretty colour of the bricks, set this Regency style house apart. It is an architectural jewel of which Port Elgin can be proud.

It boasts a classical Doric porch with a delicate iron railing above. In the spirit of 19th century eclecticism, a gothic element is added by the presence of a kingpin in the gable.

Jesse Shier (1838-1916) was, at one time, a partner in the town's major industry (established in 1883), The Port Elgin Brush Co. He later operated Shier's drugstore.

Saugeen Township

The Charles Thede House   1878 (name and date stone)
Saugeen Township   S Pt Lots 11,12,13, Con 8   N Pt Lots 11,12,13 Con 7

Charles Thede, born in 1830, and his wife Fredericka Brandt, born in 1836, came from Germany and married in Roseville near Kitchener. The township history, *Roots and Branches of Saugeen,* describes the making of their home in Saugeen. The bricks came from the Mill Creek brickyard. They planted maples along the lane and the roadway. And in their orchard they grew cherries, plums, pears and apples. Their six sons and five daughters grew up in this spacious house.

Land records show that a considerable amount of property in Saugeen Township, including this farmland, was acquired in the 1850s and 1860s by Benjamin Schantz. Charles Thede and his family came here in the early 1870s. In the Thede family history written by Jean (Thede) de Boer we read; "Charles was an ambitious man who wanted to be a landowner and would eventually acquire five fine farms all east of Port Elgin. All the sons but one followed in their father's footsteps by taking up farming. Charles did not make it easy for his sons as they had to apprentice for five years under their father before a farm was transferred. He often said to them with no uncertainty – if you do not stick with me you get nothing."

Their Gothic Revival style house is unusual in its three-gable design. These gables are high and narrow and are punctuated with dropped finials. Brickwork, centred by projected keystones above the upper front windows, outlines the gently curved and pointed arches. The name-and-date stone is tucked into the centre gable above the window. The front porch is not original.

THE DONALD CAMERON HOUSE   C.1880

Saugeen Township   Part Lot 15   Concession 5

An 1851 map of Saugeen township shows Donald Cameron in possession of this lot. The Patent from the Crown was registered in 1875 and the land remained in the Cameron name until 1945. Colonel Cameron, a lifelong bachelor, rejoiced in his honorary title and in his Scottish heritage. He became well known in the community for annual garden parties which he hosted on the spacious lawns of his estate for the members of St. Andrew's Church-Saugeen. The music was supplied by the Kincardine Pipe Band and the food was legendary, both for its quality and its quantity. Ten pies were a minimum contribution from each household we are told by Harold Sutherland in his memoir in the township history, *Roots and Branches of Saugeen.*

The house itself appears to have been built in stages with the hipped roof structure coming first. The L-shaped massing of the structure is enlivened with plenty of decorative gingerbread, artfully painted in two colours. Mature trees, as is always the case, add their softening and framing effect.

The Peter McArthur House   c.1875

Saugeen Township   Lot 34   Concession 1

An 1852 map of Saugeen Township shows lots 29 to 35 on Concession 1 belonging to the members of one Scottish immigrant family – Malcolm, Murdoch, Margaret, Lauchlen and Peter McArthur. Peter received the Crown Patent to his land in 1859. He was referred to locally as "Peter the Gold" since he had participated in the Caribou Gold Rush and reputedly made his fortune there. The large barn was built first, followed by the eleven room brick house. Each of the five bedrooms had a closet. One room, designated as a bathroom, was fitted with copper pipes. Closets and bathrooms were unusual amenities in those days. A cooperage and a sawmill were built on the property.

The style of the house is a not uncommon and effective combination of Italianate and Gothic Revival. The gables with their bargeboard and kingpins refer to the gothic while the tower and round-headed windows refer to the architecture of Tuscan villas in the 16th century – the Italianate style.

Peter McArthur and his wife had two sons and four daughters. Their sons, Archibald and John, we are told in the township history, *Roots and Branches of Saugeen*, became Members of Parliament from Alberta. Peter died in 1881 and his wife in 1895. John inherited the property and it was rented to the Thomas Switzer family for many years. Community dances were held in the great house. Its main front room was large enough to hold three squares for square dancing, and it was not uncommon for one hundred people to attend.

Southampton

"BELLEVUE" THE MCNABB/TOLMIE HOUSE C.1868
Southampton   370 Alice Street

Alexander McNabb, the builder of this house, was a truly outstanding early settler of Bruce County. His services to the community are legendary.

Descended from an ancient Highland family which settled in Lower Canada in the 1790s, he was born October 7th, 1809 at The Cedars, Soulanges County. After receiving a suitable education, he was employed by Colonel Bye in 1827 during the construction of the Rideau Canal. He went on to work in a Kingston branch of the Commercial Bank. In 1841 he became an accountant in the Crown Land's Office at Kingston. After filling this position for ten years McNabb came to Southampton in 1851 to act as a Crown Land Agent for the County of Bruce. Norman Robertson in the *History of the County of Bruce* writes, "The thirty-one years of his connection with the County of Bruce were marked by a conscientious attention to the duties of his office. Many difficult disputes regarding squatters' rights came before him, as well as attempts made by speculators to avoid the actual settlement required by statute, which Mr. McNabb settled strictly on their merits."

McNabb was the first reeve of Saugeen Township, Indian commissioner for nearly twenty-five years, an officer of the First Frontenac militia and a member of the Natural History Society of Canada.

The Rev. Major James C. Tolmie (1862-1938) bought the estate in 1920 for $3,300. He was the son of the Rev. Andrew Tolmie, Southampton's first Presbyterian minister and an occupant of the Adair/Tolmie House across the street. James Tolmie was a graduate in arts and law from Toronto University College and Knox College in 1885, and was ordained in 1889. He married Margaret Ferguson of Fergus and they had two daughters. He was both reeve and mayor of Southampton for various periods between 1926 and 1938 and served as a chaplain during WWI. Tolmie became a Liberal Member of the Legislature for Windsor and later retired to Southampton.

This is a two-storey house with a hipped roof – a vernacular style brought to Canada originally by the Loyalists. It is sometimes referred to as Wilderness Georgian. The second-storey projecting frontispiece is surmounted by a pediment. In this house, fortunately, the original entrance and verandah still exist. The unusual addition to one side was built much later.

"Gawsworth" The Smith/Fitton House   1907

Southampton   107 High Street

George E. Smith built this house for his family in 1907. He was a successful timber merchant and ship owner. More than one hundred years ago, he bought a vessel that had been wrecked at Red Bay on the Bruce Peninsula. He had it raised, repaired, and brought to Southampton, where he renamed it the *Lillie Smith*.

In 1921 the house was sold to the Bell family. T.J. Bell and Sons of Wingham had bought the Southampton Furniture Company and renamed it the Bell Furniture Company. In 1936 the Fitton-Parker Furniture Company Limited bought out Bell Furniture and operated the factory until it was sold to Sklar-Peppler in 1969.

Horace C. M. Fitton, who at one time served as mayor of Southampton, acquired the house from the Bells in 1937. Family legends maintain that an ancestor, Mary Fitton, lady-in-waiting to Queen Elizabeth I, was the alleged "dark lady" in Shakespeare's *Sonnets*. During the encumbancy of four generations of Fittons, the upper verandah was enclosed for a sunroom and a large addition to the south was built to provide a coach house/garage. The family gave the house the name of *Gawsworth* after the 14th century Fitton ancestral manor in Gawsworth, Cheshire, England.

Like its red brick Queen Anne Revival counterpart next door (page 151) this is a "grand" house. Its most prominent feature is the two-storey bandstand verandah with a conical roof. It extends the space of the house and adds to its presence. The easy architectural manipulation of motifs and materials marks the Queen Anne style which first appeared in Canada in the late 1870s and the early 1880s and remained popular until the outbreak of WW II. (The name Queen Anne is something of a misnomer since the style is only loosely based on the architecture of the era of Queen Anne.)

"ANGLICAN RECTORY" THE HAMILTON/HUSTON HOUSE C.1865
Southampton   79 Albert Street North

Frederick Proudfoot, a barrister and attorney at law, advertised in the County of Bruce 1867 directory, "5,000 acres of wild land and improved farms for sale. Money to lend on real estate." Frederick, born in 1839, had come with his parents to Southampton sometime between 1852 and 1861. Land records show that he bought this property in 1867 from William Hamilton.

It is a diminutive but distinguished example of classical Georgian styling. The windows are generous in size and quantity. The roof is gabled at each end and the closed external entry, as in Southampton's *Matheson House* (page 161), is an appropriate repetition of the classicism of the house itself. Fortunately, the wooden siding has not been reclad, the sad fate of so many fine old houses.

In 1885 Frederick Proudfoot sold the house to the Diocese of Huron for use as a rectory. The Canadian poet and Anglican clergyman, William Wilfred Campbell ("Along the line of smoky hills, the crimson forest stands . . .") lived here in 1890-91. A parish history written by the Rev. J. Fenton reads, "For a brief period this well-known Canadian poet acted as Rector of St. Paul's. Mr. Campbell was ordained in the United States. He left the parish in 1891, also the ministry of the Anglican Church. He received a civil service appointment in Ottawa and devoted himself to the cultivation of the Muse. He died in the 1920s."

George Clifton Huston and his wife became owners of the property in 1930. He was an esteemed educator after whom the local elementary school is named. Their daughter, Marjorie Chisholm, is the present incumbent.

"DUNDAS COTTAGE"   C.1882
Southampton   97 Grosvenor Street South

This buff brick cottage was the home of James Dundas (1845-1911) who was born in Enniskillen, Ireland and came to Canada in 1848. His father was an officer in the British Army who served in India. In 1869 Dundas joined the civil service as a railway mail clerk and came to Southampton in 1872. He was married in 1876 to Christina Lee (1853-1931) who had arrived in Southampton with her English parents, Mr. and Mrs. John Lee, in the late 1850s.

Dundas Cottage epitomizes the use of decorative ornamentation in heritage houses. The building itself is simple and functional. It is a cube with a hipped or four-sided roof, and appropriate openings. But consider what has been added. There is gothic flavoured bargeboard in the gable which houses a circular window to the attic. There is a commodious verandah with bracketted columns and delicate spindles. Shutters on the windows and an old-fashioned screen door add their flourish. And, surmounting the truncated roof is the prettiest belvedere on this side of Lake Huron.

THE A. F. BOWMAN HOUSE   c.1895
Southampton   125 High Street

The builder of this house was Albert Frederick Bowman, son of Isaac Erb Bowman who, with Henry Zinkan, was the owner of tanneries in Southampton, Port Elgin and St. Jacobs. The Southampton tannery, built in 1880, burned in 1900, throwing 100 men out of work. As it was not rebuilt its destruction was a serious blow to the town.

The Isaac Erb Bowman family came originally from Switzerland to Pennsylvania and from there to St. Jacobs in Upper Canada. Two sons, Albert Frederick and Charles M. came on to Southampton. The brothers and their father were involved in the founding of Mutual Life of Canada. Locally, Alfred Frederick Bowman was noted for his enthusiasm for the baseball team which he transported to out-of-town games in his two Packards.

The Queen Anne Revival style of architecture enlivens our environment. This house is a wonderful example, replete with decorated gables, advancing and receding walls, two-storey verandah, steep roof lines with intersecting ridges, and decorative chimney stacks. Almost all the tricks of the architectural trade of the time are to be found here. Moreover, the house is not crowded on its site. Lawns, shrubs and trees frame the picture of a house designed in the grand manner.

THE ADAIR/TOLMIE HOUSE   c.1869

Southampton   357 Alice Street

Thomas Adair was one of the first settlers in Bruce County, coming to Brant Township in 1849. Norman Robertson in his *History of the County of Bruce* writes, "Adair was born in 1826 just north of Glasgow, Scotland. He and his family emigrated to Canada in 1844 and settled near Peterborough. In the spring of 1849 he came to Bruce County to see what the free grants were like." He acquired four lots in Brant, did some clearing and built a shanty with his brother, John. They returned to Peterborough for the winter. The next spring Adair brought the whole family to the shanty. He continued to acquire land, improve it and then sell it. In 1857 he came to Southampton and worked for the merchant, James Calder.

Adair went from strength to strength, as a grain buyer and then as a contractor on the Southampton piers. For ten years he was reeve of the village council and was active in bringing the railway to Southampton. In 1870 he was in charge of the teamsters who accompanied the Red River Expedition. Adair was a gifted singer, a Presbyterian, a Liberal and the father of thirteen children. He died in Toronto in 1901 and is buried in Southampton.

Thomas Adair bought this property in 1864 and built this fine brick house soon after. It is typically Georgian in style – a symmetrical cube with a low hipped roof. The brickwork includes a raised stringcourse to define the change from the first to the second storey, raised quoins on the corners of the building and segmental heads over the windows. The present verandah, with its handsome pillars, bargeboard and classical centre pediment, is a close copy of an earlier verandah.

The property was sold to the Tolmie family in 1885. The Rev. Andrew Tolmie, a Presbyterian minister, had come to Southampton in 1862 where he served his congregation for over thirty-five years. A daughter, Agnes, became a prominent career woman. She was appointed Chief Observer of the Dominion Meteorological Observatory in 1917 and was presented with the Order of The British Empire by King George VI on his visit to Canada in 1939.

THE ANKENMANN OCTAGONAL COTTAGE C.1910
Southampton   65 Wellington

Peter McGregor, listed in the County of Bruce 1867 directory as a shoemaker, received the Crown Patent for this property in 1873. However it was not until 1910 that this cottage was built.

Its builder, Christopher R. Ankenmann, was the owner of a furniture company in Chesley. He became president of the Furniture Section of the Canadian Manufacturers' Association.

This is surely one of the most delightful cottages anywhere. It is set amongst trees only steps from the beach on Lake Huron. The tower not only provides sleeping space but also a lookout onto the lake. Roomy two-storey porches enlarge the cottage's living space. And all is painted crisp white with scarlet trim.

THE CAPTAIN JOHN SPENCE HOUSE   C.1853

Southampton   18 Huron Street North

Captain John Spence (1814-1904) was born in Birsay, Pomono Island, Orkney. In his early years, he served on a Greenland sailing ship and was apprenticed as a boat builder at Stromness in the Orkneys. In Canada he and his companion, Captain William Kennedy (born in 1814, the son of Alexander Spence, the Chief Factor of Cumberland House on the Saskatchewan River, and Aggathas, a Cree woman) signed up with the Hudson's Bay Company – Spence about 1835 and Kennedy in 1833 – sailing and building boats in northern Canada. They both resigned from HBC in 1846 in a dispute over company policy of selling liquor to the Indians.

The two friends came together to Southampton via a trail from Sydenham – later named Owen Sound – in June 1848. Spence erected a log cabin near the mouth of the Saugeen river. He married Jane Harold in Kingston in 1850 and brought her back to Southampton where they built their home. Spence and Kennedy worked together as fishermen, purchasing the Niagara Fish Company from Dr. "Tiger" Dunlop and his associates in Goderich – an unsuccessful venture. Kennedy was chosen by Lady Franklin in 1851 to command the *Prince Albert*, a ninety-ton brig with a crew of eighteen, in search of the doomed Franklin Party in the Arctic. As a young boy in 1819-20, Kennedy had met John Franklin at Cumberland House.

Spence commenced trading along the coast of Lake Huron and Georgian Bay. He had a long and distinguished career carrying freight and passengers by schooner. In 1876 he and his crew saved fifteen shipwrecked sailors off the coast of Michigan, receiving a gold watch from United States President Ulysses S. Grant in gratitude. In 1895 he lost his youngest son, Alexander Peter, in a tragic accident while on a sailing trip to Detroit. He and his wife had also raised John Jr., Mary, James Hendry, David William, and Margaret Eleanor. All four sons were Great Lakes ship captains.

The Spence house is of frame construction covered with wooden siding. Somewhat later it was covered with roughcast. The architectural style is commonly known as Regency, characterized by a generous centre entrance with sidelights, large symmetrically placed windows and, in this case, a massive hipped roof which overhangs the front verandah.

This small building holds the history of the founder of Southampton and his family within its walls. It is the place from which the town grew and marine history over a large part of Lake Huron was shaped. Men and women such as John and Jane Spence lived lives rich in adventure, courage and honour.

THE SOLOMON KNECHTEL HOUSE 1897
Southampton   106 Victoria Street

Solomon Knechtel, brother of Daniel Knechtel who founded the Knechtel Furniture Company of Durham, was an inventor of wood-turning and other furniture making machinery. His frame house is a remarkable example of the turner's art. The style of the large two-and-a-half storey structure must have been in the height of fashion when it was built. It features recessed balconets in two gables which are emphasized by spiral turned columns. Large, elaborate, double brackets call attention to the intersecting roof lines. The massive verandah displays triple columns and well-articulated balusters and railings.

Sol came to Southampton in 1889 as manager of a newly opened branch of the Knechtel Furniture Company. The S. M. Knechtel Chair Factory built by his nephew, and the furniture section of the Wood Turning Co. amalgamated in the early 1900s to form the Southampton Furniture Co. In 1906 the enterprising Sol Knechtel built a foundry and mattress company.

The parents of Solomon and Daniel had emigrated from Germany to Upper Canada and raised thirteen children. The sons, named after Biblical characters, were Daniel, Peter, Solomon, Jacob, Abraham, Isaac, Joshua, Abel, Ephraim and Gideon!

"Glen Huron" The Captain Dan McLeod House c.1865

Southampton   6 Huron Street North

Donald "Dan" McLeod, a local fisherman and manager of the Dominion Fish Co. operation in Southampton, lived here until his death in 1914. The Dominion Fish Co. was owned by the Booth Company of Chicago which operated another plant in Wiarton. Born in Perthshire, Scotland, McLeod came to Canada in 1863. He was noted as a skilled performer of Scottish dances.

His two-storey house is a typical example of the vernacular Georgian style in this region. The long axis of the building is the front facade in which the front entrance is centered. The roof is gabled at each end and windows are placed to reflect the symmetrical organization of the interior. An extra fillip has been added in this case – an undersized gable centred in the roof and decorated with gothicized bargeboard, kingpin and quatrefoil.

THE JOHN "SIMON" MATHESON HOUSE   C.1890

Southampton   52 Grosvenor Street

This house presents a simple but elegant front facade. With its short axis parallel to the street and a front gable with returned eaves, we are given the view of a quasi-Greek temple. The drama of the building is heightened by the stark combination of white roughcast and black trim. The enclosed entry to one side is an appropriate repetition of the whole of the front facade.

This was the home of John "Simon" Matheson, fisherman and owner of the fishing tug, *La Plante*. It is not known whether he built the house after he bought the property in 1890 or whether the house has an earlier date. Matheson lived here until his death in 1945 when his daughter took the house over. Early photographs show several sheds to the rear, where fishing gear was stored. Simon was the son of Captain Murdock Matheson, who lived in a nearby house named *Windward*, and who owned several early sailing fishing boats.

The Conaway/Forsyth House   c.1877

(with major changes in the 1920's)

Southampton   97 Huron Street South

One of Southampton's first settlers, Robert Reid, obtained this land from the Crown in 1853. He was a merchant, contractor and Southampton's first postmaster. It is thought that James T. Conaway built the original brick house here. Conaway, who had settled with his father in Arran Township about 1852, traded his farmstead for this village lot. He was warden of the Provisional Bruce County council in 1862 and reeve of Southampton in 1880. William McGregor Lambert, the Keeper of the Chantry Island Lighthouse from 1880 to 1907, became the next owner.

The house was transformed to its present form in 1924 by Georgina Forsyth, the wife of the principle owner of the Forsyth Shirt Co. in Kitchener. It was extensively enlarged and remodelled under the direction of an architect. Occupied only in the summer months, the house and the garden became a showplace for the town.

The style may be referred to as English Tudor Revival – a style of architecture popular from the 1920s until the late 1930s in Canada. It is a blend of a variety of elements of late English medieval styles, including Elizabethan and Jacobean. The style is identified by the use of steep gables, half-timbering, and mixes of stucco, stone and wood, in order to create a picturesque effect. The awning roof sweeps downward and outward to create a commodious verandah. The sweep of the roof is artfully repeated in the roof of the front dormer. The pergola is supported by sturdy stone pillars which, much to the dismay of Frederick Forsyth, cost $125 each. Their skilled stone mason, George Nickle, also created the massive stone chimney. Here is a house of distinction (historically and architecturally), surrounded by gardens and mature trees, on a superb site.

St. Edmund's Township

THE JACOB BELROSE HOUSE   1875

St. Edmund's Township   Located on St. Edmund's Township Museum Property, Tobermory

St. Edmund's Township, located at the northern tip of the Bruce Peninsula, was settled relatively late in the 19th century. The first sale of land occurred in 1870. The township history, *Hewers of the Forest, Fishers of the Lakes*, reads, "Throughout the 1800s and until WWI it was quite common to see Indian encampments at Tobermory". The native hunting reserve, a Saugeen Ojibway Nations' Territory is still to be found here. The Bruce Peninsula National Park which includes the islands off Tobermory, the former Cypress Lake Provincial Park and three Nature Reserves encompasses more than half of the territory of the township.

The remoteness of the area and relative scarcity of people provided an incentive to engage in homebrewing and bootlegging in the early years of the 20th century as evidenced by place names like *Whiskey Harbour* and *Bootleggers' Cave*.

This lowly log house was built in 1875 by Jacob Belrose (1834-1906), an immigrant from Brittany. He and his wife, Agnes Biggar, raised five sons and two daughters here. It is entirely typical of the first shelters hastily erected by settlers who were not only required by law to build a dwelling of at least eighteen by twenty-five feet, but to also immediately clear and fence 5% of their property (for which they had paid 80 cents an acre with a downpayment of 1/5 of the total). This log house was continuously occupied from 1875 until the early 1950s.

The Richards/Start House   c.1870
Tara   93 Brook Street West

This lovely house in the pretty village of Tara gains much of its appeal from its ornamental brickwork which gives definition to the walls and relieves the monotony of flat surfaces. Moreover, this house has the design bonus of advancing and retreating wall planes and a tower. The gables are enhanced with restrained bargeboard topped with finials. The house is a felicitous example of architectural eclecticism in the Victorian era. Witness the gothic gables, Italianate paired windows and di-chromatic brickwork, also the Queen Anne complexity of outline and the picturesque massing of the structure.

It was built by Thomas S. V. Richards (1834-1918) who came to Canada with his parents, Henry and Ann Richards from Cornwall in 1845-1846. He arrived in Tara about 1854 and married Ann Marie Brown in 1857. Their ten children were born between 1858 and 1881. He became a stone mason, bricklayer and building contractor and established a brick and tile yard. His father had built and operated Tara's first sawmill in 1854 and gristmill in 1857.

The Thomas Richards family, including nine of their ten children, left for western Canada in the early 1880s. He and his sons became successful contractors in Strathcona.

The next owners of the house, Charles Edward Secord Start, QC, and his wife Elizabeth, lived here for over half a century. He practiced law for seventy-five years in this village. Born in Hamilton in 1860, Start died in Tara at the age of ninety-nine years. His father, grandfather, great grandfather and son were all lawyers.

THE JAMES PURVES HOUSE   C.1880
Tara   62 Main Street

Soon after the survey of Arran Township was completed in 1851, John Hamilton and Richard Berford, early settlers in the area, located here along the Sauble River. In 1858, Berford registered a Village Plan and bought many of the town lots himself. This property was part of one of them. After passing through several hands it was purchased by James Purves, a builder and a member of the village council, in 1877. Purves built two houses side by side – this house and its twin. The twin has been so modernized that the character of the building has been lost. Fortunately, in this house we have the original.

What a charmer it is! A diminutive, domestic version of the high Victorian style referred to as Second Empire. The curving mansard roof is intact as are the classical decorative details – the pediment window hoods, the pediment shelter over the door and the pedimented dormer roofs. It is a true cottage, defined in the Oxford dictionary as " a labourer's or villager's small dwelling".

The Whitford Vandusen House   c.1875

Tara   91 Main Street

This is the house of an "important" person. H. Belden & Co.'s 1880 *Historical Atlas for Bruce County* has an illustration of the house in all its original glory. The extensive verandah with a bell-cast roof is intact, as is the belvedere with its soaring finial which straddles the roof. Today the verandah is gone and the belvedere is sadly diminished. However, the heavy window hoods, the raised brick quoins and beltcourses and the large annex behind still add to the imposing character of the house.

Bruce Miller, in his book, *TARA Before 1981* writes, "Whitford was a school teacher in Invermay from 1859 to 1863. Then he went into partnership with John Tobey, they having purchased the general store of Donald Sutherland. For the next twenty-two years he carried on a very successful business and then sold out to his brother H.A. to open Vandusen's Bank, Tara's second bank. He sold this business to the Merchants Bank of Canada in 1901." Vandusen was a member of Tara's first council and built the fifteen room British Hotel in 1883. For forty-three years he was the kingpin of Tara's business community. When he sold his bank he left Tara to go on to a larger business career in Toronto.

Walkerton

THE DICKISON/HALL HOUSE   C.1895
Walkerton   124 Colborne Street

When this house was built about 1895, one aspect of its style represented the latest thinking in domestic architecture. This is the glazing in the parlour window downstairs. The small panes of glass are found in the Arts and Crafts style – a style which followed the late Victorian. Otherwise, this strong, sober house reflects tradition in its massing and openings. It represents the best of Ontario small-town domestic architecture.

The house was built for George J. Dickison, M.D., who had come from Normanby Township in Grey County. In 1900 the property was sold to another physician, Walter Allen Hall.

Hall was born in Cromarty, Perth County, went to Normal School and taught in Bruce for almost ten years before attending Queen's University in medicine. He graduated in 1900 and came directly to Walkerton to practice. He and Clara Evelyn Bartleman had been married in 1895. Their only child died at the age of seven years. W.A. Hall was elected Liberal member to the House of Commons for South Grey in 1925 and held his seat until 1935 when he was defeated by Agnes MacPhail.

THE DONALD SINCLAIR HOUSE   c.1885

Walkerton   604 Jackson Street South

Donald Sinclair's house, like the houses we build for ourselves, represents a personal statement. The statement is: "I, the owner of this house, am a person of some standing in the community However, I am a modest man, not given to ostentation. My family home is large, well-built, functional and in the style of the day."

It is the home of a Scot born in 1829 on the island of Islay. Sinclair emigrated to Canada with his parents in 1851 and came to Bruce County in 1853. Norman Robertson, in his *History of the County of Bruce*, informs us that Sinclair worked as a teacher for some years and was elected to the post of deputy reeve of Arran Township in 1863. In 1869 he moved to the village of Paisley to run a general store. He entered provincial politics in 1867 when he was elected MLA for Bruce North and retained his seat until 1883. He became the first Speaker of the Legislature of Ontario. Isabella Adair, daughter of Thomas Adair, a prominent pioneer of Brant Township, married Donald Sinclair and they settled with their children in this Walkerton house. He became Registrar of Deeds for Bruce County. He died in the year 1900. The Sinclair house remained in the family until 1965.

THE H. P. O'CONNOR HOUSE   C.1885

Walkerton   430 Jackson Street

This expansive, white-painted , brick house is especially beautiful in the winter when its pristine quality is enhanced by a snow-covered landscape. Its plan is L-shaped, a form well known to Ontario residents. Its style is the familiar blend of Italianate – in the handsome door, the paired round-headed windows, the pediment in the verandah roof and the double brackets. It is Gothic Revival in the steeply pitched gable-end roof and bargeboard. Stacked bay windows add variety to the front facade. Interestingly, in order to preserve the symmetrical placement of the windows, false windows covered by shutters have been added.

Hamilton B. O'Connor (1817-1894) was a clerk of the Second Division court of Bruce County located in Teeswater. His son, Hamilton P. O'Connor (1844-1900) had this house built for his family around 1885. H. P. O'Connor married Jane W. McLean in 1875 and was called to the Bar in 1878. He practiced law in Walkerton with his brother, F. S. O'Connor (who lived with his family in a similar house next door). O'Connor also served as mayor of Walkerton, 1880-1881, and Liberal MLA for south Bruce from 1882-1890. At the close of his political life he was awarded the once coveted but now eliminated title of QC (Queen's Counsel).

The next owners of the house were William Gunn Owens (1869-1955) and his wife Julia Elizabeth. He came from St. Catharines, was called to the Bar in 1901 and served nineteen years as a Bruce County judge.

In 1945 George Bernard Bogdon and his wife Eileen Fisher, to whom he was married in 1941, lived here with their family. He was President and CEO of the Bogdon & Gross Furniture Company founded by his father, Peter Bogdon, in 1927 in Kitchener. The company moved to Walkerton in 1938, taking over the former Knechtel Furniture Company plant.

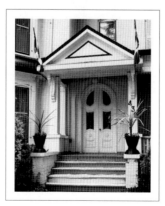

THE JOSEPH WALKER HOUSE   c.1860

Walkerton   15 McNabb Street

The most historic house in Walkerton is, of course, that built by the founder of the town, Joseph Walker. By all accounts, Walker was a vigorous, feisty gentleman. Norman Robertson writes, (*History of the County of Bruce*) "At the time he entered the county of Bruce he was a man of forty-nine years of age , stoutly and compactly built, rather below the average height, energetic, tenacious of purpose, and of an active, nervous temperament. Many of the old settlers speak warmly of him for the kindly acts extended to them in the early days, when nearly everyone was in comparatively poor circumstances."

Joseph Walker (1801-1873) was born in County Tyrone, Ireland and came to Canada in the 1820s. He and his son, William, arrived in this enchanting valley of the Saugeen River in May, 1850. They soon found the best mill site and commenced to build a dam and saw and grist mills. His first home, a log house, also served as a hotel for settlers coming up from the south. He acquired ten farm lots for the purpose of establishing a town, and built this substantial stone house and several others. He became Walkerton's first mayor and served several terms as the reeve of neighbouring Brant Township.

In 1870 the ever resourceful Joseph Walker moved to Manitoulin Island to make a fresh start. His Walkerton house became the home of Reuben E. Truax, born in 1848 in Ontario. Truax developed a prosperous saw and planing mill business on the site of the original sawmill erected by Walker. He entered politics and served as a Liberal MP from 1891 to 1896 and Liberal MLA from 1894 to 1904.

The style of the house has been waggishly described as Wilderness Georgian. Built of rubble limestone, its openings are symmetrically placed. The centre front entrance opens onto the usual centre-hall configuration of rooms. The gable-end roof has returned eaves and internal chimneys rise at either end.

THE JUDGE KLEIN HOUSE   C.1895

Walkerton   809 Yonge Street South

John Klein, born in 1826, and Sophia Amelia (1852-1894) came from Alsace with their children to Walkerton in 1870. Here, he established Walkerton's first newspaper, "Die Glocke" (in German). Their son Alphonse and his wife Clara Elizabeth, lived in this interesting Queen Anne Revival house. Alphonse Klein, a well-known and respected barrister, was appointed judge of the county court in 1893.

Library files in Walkerton suggest that the original building on the property was a small, woodframe house, later enlarged and veneered with brick. The house and nearby coach house are considerably enhanced by their situation on a large lot with mature trees. A corner tower, an upper balcony snugged into the swooping roof, and an expansive verandah add appeal to the total design.

THE LIPPERT HOUSE   C.1876

Walkerton   208 Mary Street

This picturesque fieldstone house is unique in Walkerton. Although its size appears diminutive from the street, the back elevation is a full two storeys in height. The house has been built on a slope – always a good idea if an appropriate slope can be found! Highly coloured small stones have been chosen by the mason for the body of the structure, while much larger stones have been used to mark the corners. Segmented stone voussoirs over the windows have been fashioned by hand. The hipped roof is unusual in that it has been truncated at the sides to allow for returned eaves – a design bonus.

A vernacular version of the Regency style, the house was built for Frederick (1851-1930) and Rebecca Lippert, both from Waterloo County, who came to Walkerton in 1876. He became owner of a monument business and served as councillor, reeve and mayor of the town over a period of seventeen years. His son, Frederick Jr., also lived here with his wife, Catherine Seyffert. Fred Jr. followed in his father's footsteps, both in the monument business and in municipal affairs. He, in his time, also served as councillor, reeve and mayor.

THE WILLIAM SHORTT HOUSE   C.1880
Walkerton   505 Colborne Street

One of the few recorded reprobates of Bruce County was the first owner of this property. He was James G. Cooper, born in England in 1839, arriving in Bruce County in 1858. By the time he was thirty-five years old he had been appointed treasurer of both the town and the county. He also worked as a loan and insurance agent. In the early 1880s Cooper became a lieutenant-colonel in the 32nd Bruce Battalion. But it all ended in 1887 when he fled the country leaving an unexplained loss of $25,701 from the coffers of Bruce County.

Ironically, in 1876, the next owner and builder of this exemplary house was the Rev. William Shortt, rector of St. Thomas Church. In 1899, Duncan Trail, a hardware merchant in Walkerton, bought the house. A later, long-term owner was Harry Alton, principal of the Walkerton Public School from 1921 to 1957, and a judge of the Juvenile Court.

The house is a relatively pure example of the Italianate style, popular in the 1880s in urban Ontario. The advancing centre bay defines the building. The handsome doorway is given a classical treatment with a shallow pediment supported by brackets, over dentil moulding. Pilasters flank the panelled two-leaf door. Double windows above are protected by a matching pediment which neatly fits into a shallow gable in the roof. Decorative roof brackets, fine brickwork and conforming window shutters complete the picture of an elegant town house.

THE JOHN ROWLAND HOUSE   C.1900
Walkerton   410 Jackson Street South

The *Walkerton Walking Tour* brochure describes this house as, "the best unaltered example of the Queen Anne Revival style in Bruce County." It is indeed an important house built of the finest materials by skilled craftsmen in a congenial style. The architect was Rob Gray from Harriston.

The red brick masonry is of a high order, sills and lintels are made of stone, gables are shingled and the verandah has panelled posts and well-turned balusters above and slender turned columns below. The size and complexity of the building with its wide two-storey bay windows and intersecting rooflines confers a presence of wealth and stability.

John Rowland, who died in 1949, has been described as a financier and cattle buyer. It is believed that he had the house built for his daughter on her marriage. The house remained in the family until well into the second half of the twentieth century.

The James Warren House   c.1890
Walkerton   222 Colborne Street South

Two generations of the Warren family have lived in this accommodating Victorian house. James Warren (1837-1917), born in Halton County, was trained as a teacher and then as a Dominion land surveyor. In the early years of his career, his work took him throughout the northwest from Winnipeg to the Rockies. Later he settled his family in Kincardine and then moved to Walkerton in 1895. Here, one of his civic-minded activities was to chair the library board which arranged for a Carnegie library to be built in 1914.

The daughters of the family – Agnes and Winnifred Warren and Ruth McBurney – continued to occupy the family home at various stages of their lives. Winnifred came here after her retirement as a missionary teacher in North Honan, China. One of her students there was Dr. Robert McClure, future moderator of the United Church of Canada.

The house presents a classical facade to the street. Particularly notable are the returned eaves of the front gable which, with the roof of the bay window, form the illusion of a pediment. Great use is made of bay windows in the houses of Walkerton. In this case, a major two-storey , six-window bay defines the front elevation of the house.

THE USSHER/FAREWELL HOUSE C.1867

Walkerton   202 Catherine Street

The names of Henry Ussher MD and his wife Catherine, first owners of this admirable house, appear in census and directory records from 1866 until 1880. He is described as being of Irish descent and born in 1837 in Quebec.

The house then became home and office for Dr. Adolphus Farewell and his wife. Their daughter Minnie (1891-1983) continued to live here until her death. She worked as a town librarian for many years.

The Regency style cottage is raised on a high foundation to provide room for the doctor's office and surgery in the lower level. A separate, closed entrance to the lower level is seen on the left of the photograph. The house is of frame construction covered with roughcast which has been scored to give the impression of ashlar (smooth-cut blocks of stone). Tall, narrow windows are its distinctive feature. The hipped roof is steeply pitched and punctuated by two dormers. Their roofs repeat the lines of the verandah pediment over the front door. Dentil moulding lines the eaves.

This house is an exceptionally well-executed vernacular version of the Regency style and, as such, is a significant part of the architectural heritage of Walkerton.

"Fairbairn" The James Paterson Jr. House   1886
(date marker in the chimney)
Wiarton   285 Mary Street (at Gould Street)

James Gilmore Paterson Sr. (1820-1886) was born in Paisley, Scotland and trained as a chemist there. At the end of the Crimean War in 1856 a depression settled over Scotland which precipitated the immigration of a large number of Scots to Canada – among them James Paterson, with his wife and small family. They landed in Toronto in the spring of 1857 where he worked for Lyman Bros. & Co., a wholesale and retail drug firm, until he felt that the city air was adversely affecting his health. He escaped to Colpoy's Village in the fall of 1861 – not far from Wiarton. As one of the first settlers in the area, his services and those of his wife, Margaret, trained in midwifery at the Toronto School of Medicine, were in constant demand. Paterson opened a drug store in Wiarton in 1869 and he and his family became prosperous and valued citizens of the town.

This house, built by their son, James Jr. (1849-1937)), and named after his wife, Jessie Fairbairn (1855-1938), is an ornament to Wiarton. It is a large house built of buff brick trimmed in contrasting red brick. The sunrise motif above the verandah pediment, windows and gable, and the interior fittings engraved with rush bundles, reflect the late Victorian penchant for all things Japanese. Its strong presence emerges from its multiple rooflines, ornamental chimneys and above all, its three-sided verandah highlighted by delicate bargeboard and slender posts.

"Hillcrest" The Gideon Kastner House   c.1885
Wiarton   394 Gould Street

This house was built by Andrew Charles Kyle, a prominent hardware and house furnishings merchant in Wiarton. An unconfirmed anecdote has it that Kyle gave the house to Gideon Kastner to settle a gambling debt.

Kastner (1865-1949) was the energetic son of immigrant parents from Alsace-Lorraine. He was born in Sebringville, Perth County into a family of ardent followers of William Lyon Mackenzie. Gideon came to the Wiarton area in 1886 when he purchased his first sawmill near Clavering. When the Jones Mill in Wiarton burned in 1903 he purchased the site along with the Ely Woodworking Factory. With David Porter he constructed the town wharf and, later, eleven wharves and breakwaters throughout Georgian Bay. Kastner managed the Wiarton Furniture Factory for many years, was councillor, reeve, mayor, president of the Bruce County Liberal Association and, ultimately, warden of Bruce County.

This late Victorian house poses a counterpoint to the Paterson house across the street. The corner bay, tall chimneys with projecting top courses, intersecting roof lines and dormer contribute to its visual interest. The verandah was lost in the 1960s but replaced in 1970 to the same height and pitch of the original roof.

THE MATTHEWS HOUSE   C.1878

Wiarton   666 Berford Street

Thomas Gilpin built the oldest part of this house for his sister Martha who was Wiarton's first school teacher. Gilpin owned one of Wiarton's early sawmills, a planing mill, and a sash & door factory. The house was eighteen feet by twenty-four feet, supported by log joists twelve inches in diameter.

The next owners, in 1882, were brothers John and Joseph Kidd, merchants from Simcoe and Perth counties. They added the front portion of the house in a style of the family estate in western Ontario. The generic style of the 1870s is well articulated by a large central gable, a modest entry and three pretty bay windows. The eared door hoods and sloping door frames add to the simple charm of the building. At one time, there was a balcony above the door.

During their tenure, Catholic church services were held here. They were conducted by a priest from Owen Sound who travelled to Wiarton by boat and then on to Cape Croker by horseback to hold services there. The late Bishop Kidd of the London Diocese was born in this house.

The next incumbents in 1901 were Edward Melligan, a conductor on the Grand Trunk Railway, and his wife Josephine.

Finally, in 1929, Burton and Emily Matthews, who owned a bakery in Wiarton, bought the house. They were notable for their lovely gardens and legendary hospitality. One son, Howard, moved into the house with his wife Elizabeth in 1954 and here they raised their three sons. Elizabeth, a widow, lives here still. She has lovingly documented the evolution of the house and the story of its occupants in a piece titled *666 Berford Street and its People*.

PHOTO COURTESY OF ELIZABETH MATTHEWS

"The White House" The Ames/Hough House c.1881

Wiarton N Pt Lot 10   Concession 21   Keppel Township   Grey County

This large Victorian frame house is almost hidden from public view by immense century-old Norway spruces. The house, built of yellow brick, was later covered with clapboard. It is now clad in aluminum.

The property was once part of an eighty-five acre lot Patented in 1876 by James Paterson Sr., Wiarton's legendary druggist and lay physician. It is located just outside the southern edge of Wiarton. George W. Ames (1856-1931) and his wife, Mary (1861-1896) bought the house from Paterson in 1883 for $1,500. Ames had established the G. W. Ames Bank in 1880 in Wiarton.

In 1944 the house passed into the hands of his daughter, Mabel Grace, who had married Dr. Arthur H. Hough, an 1892 graduate in medicine from Victoria University. She was widely known for her hospitality and ran the establishment as a bed & breakfast for some years. Her son, George, returned from New York and his work with A. E. Ames & Co. to retire to *The White House*. Winifred, his widow, lives there now.

THE ARTHUR JONES HOUSE   C.1870
Wiarton   Bayshore Road

Arthur Jones came to Wiarton in 1872 and operated a sawmill here. His brother, Charles Cooper Jones, had built the mill and this house nearby a few years before. When he sold both mill and house to Arthur he moved up onto the Niagara Escarpment directly above to become a "gentleman" farmer. The brothers had come from a well-connected, prosperous family which had settled earlier in the century near Guelph. They were said to be related to the Dukes of Bedford.

The stone house, which has been covered with roughcast scored to resemble ashlar, retains some of its original glazing, a side entrance, and the back shed where deer and other wild game were hung to cure.

Between 1929 and 1979 the house, which overlooks Colpoy's Bay, was run by Myrtle Langford as a hostelry and boarding house called The Anchor Inn. Her summer visitors came from far afield – New York City, Montreal, Detroit and points west.

When the north end of the main street of Wiarton was extended up over the escarpment, blasting loosened a boulder which plunged through the roof of the house. It still rests within the house today. The road up the hill became known as "Byer's Blasted Hill" after the town reeve, D. J. Byers, who initiated the project.

THE CAPTAIN JOHN FREDERICK DAVIS HOUSE   C.1900

Wiarton   346 Berford Street

Captain Davis, a master with the Canada Steamship Line who died in 1963, piloted the first British ship to pass through the St. Lawrence Seaway to the head of the Great Lakes in April, 1959. He also once held the record for the fastest time piloting a ship through the Welland Canal. He married Eleanor Paterson, a young school teacher in Wiarton. They bought this house in 1920 and lived here with their family until the late 1960s.

The winged brackets which support the wide eaves of the house at the corners above diagonal wall planes are a widely used design element in this area. Advancing and retreating wall planes, generous windows and superior brickwork, including the corbelled chimney, are notable. Finally, massive attic-level bays in the form of classical pediments lend an air of importance to this Queen Anne Revival house.

THE CHARLES RECKIN HOUSE   C.1900

Wiarton   330 Berford Street

Another of the grand houses on "Prosperity Hill" in Wiarton was built by Charles Reckin (1850-1926). He was born in Germany and came with his parents to Neustadt, Grey County at the age of four. In 1875 he married Rosina Kabel of Waterloo County and they had five children. Reckin became the proprietor of the St. Alban's Hotel and also worked as a building contractor. He owned and operated the stone flour and grist mill in Wiarton – now converted to a restaurant and offices.

Reckin's house, which is slated for rehabilitation, was the talk of the town when it was built around the turn of the century. Virtuoso brickwork wraps the north front facade in a wide curve creating a tower with a conical roof. A suspended, glazed turret capped with a pagoda roof, at the other front corner of the house balances this massive tower. Reckin placed a piece of granite in a niche beside the second floor door which sparkles in the morning sun. The heavy front porch may be a later addition.

THE JAMES SYMON HOUSE C.1890

Wiarton   376 Berford Street

The Wiarton dry goods business, Wm. A. Symon & Sons, was established in 1878 by a forty-two year old Aberdeenshire man, William Symon. James Symon, one of William's three sons and the builder of this house, carried on the business after his father's death in 1910. James was a leading citizen of Wiarton – serving as councillor for many years and as mayor.

Located on the south end of Wiarton's main street in what was originally the Greenlees survey, and which later came to be affectionately known as "Prosperity Hill", the house is a restrained example of the Queen Anne Revival style in Canadian architecture. Here the effect depends upon the skillful manipulation of steep roof lines and intersecting ridges. Bays with decorative barge board and stained glass windows add interest to the composition.

GLOSSARY

ashlar. Squared, cut stone laid in regular courses with fine joints.

aesthetic period. A late 19th century movement in the decorative arts and architecture in which exotic, particularly Japanese, motifs were used. Associated with the Arts & Crafts movement.

balustrade. A series of turned uprights supporting a railing.

bargeboard. Decoratively carved boards attached under the sloping gable ends of a roof. Also known as gingerbread.

bay. A window, door, or other opening, comprising one division of a facade.

bellcast. Bell-shaped or flared eaves of a roof.

beltcourse. See stringcourse.

belvedere. A glazed structure projecting above a roof, affording a good view, or lighting an attic. Sometimes referred to as a monitor or lantern.

clapboard. Horizontal wood cladding of overlapping boards.

common bond. Five rows of stretchers (the long side of the brick), one row of headers (the short end of the brick) repeated throughout.

corbel. A supporting projected brick or stone, sometimes a repetitive decoration.

cornice. Ornamental moulding which projects along the top of a wall or building.

crocket. One of a series of carved projections decorating the sloping sides of spires, pinnacles, gables.

cruciform. Cross-shaped.

dentil. A small, tooth-like block, used in a row as a decorative feature in a cornice.

dormer. A window that projects from a sloping roof with a roof of its own.

entablature. The horizontal component that lies directly above a column or wall; in classical architecture, the upper part of an order, consisting of architrave, frieze and cornice.

extrados. The outer curved face of an arch.

finial. A pointed ornament crowning a gable, pediment or roof.

frieze. A wide, often decorated horizontal band at the top of a wall; in classical architecture, between the architrave and the cornice.

frontispiece. The main facade of a building or its principal entrance bay.

gable. The triangular portion at the end of a pitched roof. It may be straight-sided or shaped, as in a Dutch gable.

Georgian style. Named after the English monarchs of the 18th and early 19th century, modeled on the clear proportions, symmetry and repetition of Greek and Roman classical buildings. Local variations of the style are referred to as "Wilderness Georgian".

Gothic Revival style. Refers to a late 18th century and 19th century revival of the picturesque, medieval cathedral architecture of England, France and other European countries.

hipped roof. Roof rising from all four sides of a building.

Italianate style. Derived from the villa architecture of Tuscany, Italy.

kingpin. A vertical carved post rising from the apex of a gable.

label. A rectangular moulding above a window or door which throws off the rain and snow.

lintel. The horizontal member supporting the wall above a door or window.

lug sill. The lower, horizontal member which extends beyond the vertical sides of a window frame, as opposed to a slip sill which is flush.

mansard roof. Has a double slope, the upper nearly flat, the lower steep and often curved; named after Francois Mansart, a 17th century French architect.

neo-classic style. Inspired from the architectural ruins of ancient Greece and Rome; popular in Canada from the late 1700s to around the 1850s.

ogee. A double-curved line made up of a convex and concave part.

oculus. A circular opening in a wall or ceiling.

Ontario house or cottage. The generic domestic architectural style of Ontario; one or one-and-a-half storeys in height with a pitched roof and a centre-front gable and symmetrically placed openings.

Palladian style. Derived from the buildings and publications of the architect of the 16th century, Andrea Palladio.

pediment. Triangular decoration above doors, windows, porches or building fronts.

pilaster. An ornamental half-column projecting slightly from a wall.

quatrefoil. Four-lobed ornament.

Queen Anne Revival style. Very popular in Canada in the late 19th century among the prosperous middle-class. Characterized by towers, complex rooflines, varied materials.

quoin. Squared members at the corner of a wall, usually laid alternately with small and large faces; usually decorative.

Regency cottage. In Ontario a ground-hugging, square, hip-roofed structure with a centre hall plan.

Regency. In architecture the period from about the 1790s to about 1840.

Richardsonian Romanesque. Named after the American architect, Henry Hobson Richardson, for his personal style – a massive, powerful, round-arched adaptation of the architecture of 10th century Europe.

roughcast. An exterior plaster "cast" by hand onto the exterior of a building.

Second Empire style. Most easily recognized by the mansard or broken roof combined with a rich, classicizing treatment of the exterior.

sidelight. A window beside a door, forming part of the door unit.

solid brick. Brick masonry supplies the supporting structure of a building. Walls will be two or more layers of brick in depth as opposed to a veneer of brick over a frame building.

Stick style. An American style of the late 19th century in which boards (sticks) are used to outline openings and corners – and to provide other carpenter-like, decorative details in a house.

stringcourse. Horizontal band on a masonry building usually demarking the change of storeys; a wide version is a beltcourse.

transom. A window above a door, forming a part of the door unit.

trefoil. A three-lobed ornament.

treillage. A decorative lattice-work roof support constructed of wood or metal and used in verandahs.

Tudor style. Late medieval style, elements of which reappeared in Ontario in the second half of the 19th century.

vernacular architecture. A term indicating buildings in indigenous styles from locally available materials following traditional building practice and patterns and not architect-designed.

voussoir. A brick or wedge-shaped stone forming one of the units of an arch; the central voussoir is the keystone.

Suggestions for Further Reading

GENERAL

Ashenburg, Katherine. *Going to Town: Architectural Walking Tours in Southern Ontario*. Macfarlane Walter & Ross, 1996.

Blake, Verschole Benson, and Ralph Greenhill. *Rural Ontario*. University of Toronto Press, 1969.

Brosseau, Mathilde. *Gothic Revival Architecture*. Parks Canada, 1980.

Brown, W. M. *The Queen's Bush: A Tale of the Early Days of Bruce County (1932)*. Bruce County Historical Society, 1992.

Cameron, Christina, and Janet Wright. *Second Empire Style in Canadian Architecture*. Parks Canada, 1980.

Clerk, Nathalie. *Palladian Style in Canadian Architecture*. Parks Canada, 1984.

Downing, Andrew Jackson. *The Architecture of Country Houses (1850)*. Dover, 1969.

Downing, Andrew Jackson. *Victorian Cottage Residences* (1873). Dover, 1981.

Fee, Florence A. *Pioneers in the Queen's Bush*. May 1976.

Fleming, John, Hugh Honour and Nickolaus Pevsner. The *Penguin Dictionary of Architecture*.
        Penguin books, Fourth Edition, 1991.

Fox, W. Sherwood. *The Bruce Beckons (1952)*. University of Toronto Press, 1968.

Gateman, Laura. *Echoes of Bruce County*.

Gowans, Alan. *Building Canada: An Architectural History of Canadian Life*. Oxford University Press, 1958.

Greenhill, Ralph, Ken Macpherson, and Douglas Richardson. *Ontario Towns*. Oberon, 1974.

Harrison, Gwen Smith. *A Pictorial History of Bruce County: prior to 1918*. Bruce County Historical Society, 1989.

Kalman, Harold. *History of Canadian Architecture*. 2 volumes. Oxford University Press, 1994.

Kennedy Sr., David. *Pioneer Days at Guelph and the County of Bruce (1903)*. Bruce County Historical Society, 1991.

MacRae, Marion, and Anthony Adamson. *The Ancestral Roof: Domestic Architecture of Upper Canada*.
        Clarke Irwin & Company Limited, 1963.

Mahinnick, Jean. *At Home in Upper Canada*. Clarke Irwin, 1983.

Maitland, Leslie. *Neoclassical Architecture in Canada*. Parks Canada, 1984.

Maitland, Leslie. *The Queen Anne Revival Style in Canadian Architecture*. Parks Canada 1990.

McIlwraith, Thomas. *Looking for Old Ontario: Two Centuries of Landscape Change*. University of Toronto, 1997.

McLeod, Norman. *The History of the County of Bruce: 1907-1968*. The Bruce County Historical Society, 1969.

Owen Sound Herald. *The Herald's Magazine of Industry*. c.1911.

Rempel, John. *Building With Wood*. University of Toronto Press, 1972.

Robertson, Norman. *History of the County of Bruce (1906)*. The Bruce County Historical Association, 1988.

Weichel, John. *Skeely Skipper*. Bruce County Museum & Archives, 1998.

Wright, Janet. *Architecture of the Picturesque in Canada*. Parks Canada, 1984.

Individual Townships, Towns and Villages

The following are listed by title, alphabetically, and may be found in the Bruce County Museum and Archives, Southampton, Ontario.

A History of the Township of Brant: 1854-1979.

Albemarle: A History of the Township. 1991.

All Our Yesterdays: a History of Culross Township, 1854-1984.

An Historic Album of Paisley. 1974.

Benchmarks – A History of Eastnor Township and Lion's Head. 1987

Between You and Me and the Gatepost: A Historic View of the Lion's Head Area. Walter Warder, 1897.

Brief Biography of Significant People of the Town of Port Elgin. 1993.

Bruce County Historical Society Yearbook: 1977. "Paisley, an Architectural Heritage". B. Eric Parker.

Bruce County Historical Society Yearbook: 1998. "The Pinkertons in Bruce". James E. Connell.

Bruce Township Tales & Trails: from Early Days to 1983. Editor, Anne Judd.

Celebrate Southampton: Past & Present. Editor, Sandy Tomlin, 1993.

Exploring the Bruce: a Driving Tour. 1980.

Families and Farms of Huron With its Hub, Ripley. 1985.

Footloose on the Bruce: a Historic Profile of the Warder Farm Family 1850 to 1995. Maitland Warder, 1995.

From Days of Yore: a Pictorial History of Chesley. Editors, Shirley & Donald McClure, 1995.

Green Meadows and Golden Sands: The History of Amabel Township. 1984.

Greenock Township History: 1856-1981. Editor, Laura M. Gateman.

Hewers of Forests, Fishers of Lakes: The History of St. Edmonds Township. 1984.

Historical Walks Through Carrick & Mildmay. 1989.

History of Wiarton & District. Percy Sims, and Mrs. C. Preston. 1961

Kincardine: Glimpses of the Past. 1980.

Kincardine: 1848-1984. 1982.

Paths of Paisley. B. Eric Parker, 1978.

Pioneer Days of the Bruce Peninsula. Jack Hilditch. 1982.

Reminiscences of Port Elgin 1874-1974.

Sesquicentennial at Kincardine 1848-1998.

Souvenir Booklet of Chesley: 1885-1948.

Tara: Before 1981. Bruce A. Miller, 1981.

The Chesley District. Clayton Schaus, 1967.

The History of Elderslie Township 1851-1977.

The History of Port Elgin. Heather Robertson.

Toil, Tears, and Triumph: a History of Kincardine Township. 1990.

OTHER RESOURCES FOR OWNERS OF HERITAGE BUILDINGS

LACAC (Local Architectural Conservation Action Committee) in your community. The Owen Sound LACAC is particularly active, has a useful library and a knowledgeable coordinator. LACAC , Tourism office, 1155 First Ave. W., Owen Sound, ON N4K 4K8. 519 371-9833 fax: 519 371-8628. Email: vacation@city.owen-sound.on.ca.

The Centre for Canadian Heritage Trades and Technology. Algonquin College, Perth Campus, 7 Craig St., Perth, ON K7H 1X7.   613 267-2859 ext. 5602. Fax: 613 267-3950. Email: rogersn@algonquinc.on.ca.

Well-Preserved: The Ontario Heritage Foundation's Manuel of Principles and Practice for Architectural Conservation. Mark Fram. The Boston Mills Press, 1992.

INDEX